Sew It in a Weekend

HOUSE of
WHITE
BIRCHES

PUBLISHERS
SINCE 1947

Sew It in a Weekend™

EDITOR	Julie Johnson
ART DIRECTOR	Brad Snow
PUBLISHING SERVICES DIRECTOR	Brenda Gallmeyer
MANAGING EDITOR	Dianne Schmidt
ASSISTANT ART DIRECTOR	Nick Pierce
COPY SUPERVISOR	Michelle Beck
COPY EDITORS	Nicki Lehman, Judy Weatherford
TECHNICAL EDITOR	Marla Freeman
GRAPHIC ARTS SUPERVISOR	Ronda Bechinski
BOOK DESIGN	Erin Augsburger
GRAPHIC ARTISTS	Glenda Chamberlain, Edith Teegarden
PRODUCTION ASSISTANTS	Marj Morgan, Judy Neuenschwander
TECHNICAL ARTIST	Nicole Gage
PHOTOGRAPHY SUPERVISOR	Tammy Christian
PHOTOGRAPHY	Matthew Owen
PHOTO STYLIST	Tammy Steiner

Printed in China
First Printing: 2008
Library of Congress Control Number: 2007937750
Hardcover ISBN: 978-1-59217-181-1

DRGbooks.com

1 2 3 4 5 6 7 8 9

Welcome

Let's face it. We feel passionate about our love of sewing. Whether we sew for ourselves, for gift giving or for our home, we love the feel and texture of fine fabrics; the thrill of designing, creating and using our sewn projects; and perhaps best of all, the anticipated compliments received. Sewing, to us, is creative expression at its very best.

Unfortunately, we are also very busy with obligations that may be time-consuming, sometimes energy draining, but always demanding our time and attention.

"Let your passion for sewing flow into these designs."

Sew It in a Weekend was developed to give you simple-to-sew projects that can be completed in short amounts of time, finished in hours instead of days. Projects are designed to let you enjoy your fabric stash, create fantastic fashions, glorious gifts and dynamic home decor and, of course, to keep the compliments coming!

And we all know that after a few hours spent in our sewing haven, we'll emerge renewed and refreshed, ready, once again, to take on our busy lifestyle.

So, take an hour or two to indulge yourself. Let your passion for sewing flow into these designs, and remember that even though you may be busy with other obligations, you can always return to this book to spend a few moments browsing and planning, or a blissful hour or two sewing another spectacular creation.

I know you're busy, so stop reading and start looking through this book to find your next creative project.

Until next time,

Julie

Contents

Fabulous Fashions

57

50

Glorious Gifts

Dynamic Home Decor

30

132

Fabulous Fashions

Fashion is about self-expression. Express yourself with these simple-to-sew and easily embellished wearables to create a statement that is so totally you. Have fun with these designs, be flippant or flirty or simply feel fabulous, but don't give your designer tips away. You'll have too much fun keeping your friends guessing where you shop.

Apron Duo

Designs by Lorine Mason

Fast and fun, this apron is useful for even the most basic of cooks. Whether worn while heating up leftovers, opening take-out containers or creating a multiple-course dinner, these coordinating aprons will always complement the chefs.

Apron

Estimated Time
2½ hours

Finished size
One size fits most

Materials for both
- 44/45-inch-wide mediumweight cotton fabric:
  - 1 yard floral
  - 1 yard stripe
  - 1 yard check
- 1-inch metal clip-style fastener
- 1-inch metal D ring
- Basic sewing supplies and equipment

Cutting
From floral fabric:
- Cut one 18 x 32-inch piece on fold of fabric. Referring to diagram (Figure 1) cut floral apron.
- Cut one 3-inch strip the width of the fabric for pocket tabs and binding.

4"

17"

Cut On Fold

32"

18"

Figure 1

From stripe fabric:
• Cut one 18 x 32-inch piece on fold of fabric for stripe apron. Referring to Figure 1, cut stripe apron.
• Cut one 9 x 10-inch rectangle. Referring to Figure 2 (below), cut upper pocket for floral apron.
• Cut one 23 x 9½-inch rectangle for lower pocket on floral apron.
• Cut one 3 x 10-inch strip on the bias of the fabric for binding.

From check fabric:
• Cut one 9 x 10-inch rectangle. Referring to Figure 2, cut upper pocket for stripe apron.

Figure 2

• Cut one 23½ x 9¼-inch rectangle for lower pocket on stripe apron.
• Cut seven 3-inch strips the width of the fabric for straps and binding.

Binding
Join like strips of fabric together using a ¼-inch diagonal seam. Press each joined strip in half with wrong sides together, matching long edges; open strip and press raw edges toward center fold and press. Fold on center fold and press.

Assembly
Note: *Instructions are given for floral apron, with instructions for stripe apron in parentheses.*

Use ½-inch-wide seam allowances unless otherwise stated.

1. Cut two 5-inch lengths from floral binding strip for pocket tab. Slip D ring (clip fastener) onto tab; fold tab in half. Set aside.

2. Bind top edges of upper pocket with checked (stripe) binding. Bind top edges of lower pocket with checked (floral) binding. Turn under side and bottom edges of both pockets ½ inch; press.

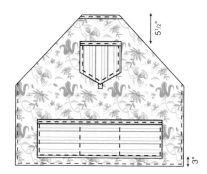

3. Referring to Figure 3, position upper pocket on apron front. Pin ends of pocket tab under bottom point of pocket. Topstitch ¼ inch from side and bottom edges, catching ends of pocket tab in stitching.

Figure 3

4. Position lower pocket on apron front (Figure 3) and topstitch ¼ inch from side and bottom edges. Stitch across pocket 7 inches from each end to divide pocket.

5. Bind the top edge of the apron with stripe (floral) binding.

6. Turn under and stitch a 1-inch hem across bottom of apron and a ¾-inch hem on each lower side.

7. Cut a 104-inch length of checked binding. Mark center of binding with a pin. Beginning 11 inches from the marked center on each side, pin binding to upper sides of apron, encasing raw edges. Topstitch binding in place, catching both turned-under binding edges when stitching, and creating ties and apron neck strap (Figure 4). ⏱

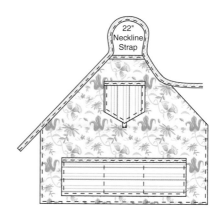

Figure 4

Reading Wrap

Design by Lorine Mason

Perfect whether thrown over your shoulders while cuddled up with a good book next to a blazing fire or used as a simple wrap on a spring evening, our version of the classic reading shawl makes a statement. Two hidden pockets add a convenient yet personal touch.

Estimated Time
2 hours

Shawl

Finished size
53 x 20½ inches

Materials
• 58–60-inch-wide fleece fabric:
  ⅔ yard print
  1 yard coordinating solid
• Basic sewing supplies and equipment

Cutting
From print fleece:
• Cut one 21 x 40-inch rectangle for wrap front.
• Cut two 21 x 7-inch rectangles for wrap ends.

From coordinating solid fleece:
• Cut one 21 x 54-inch rectangle for wrap back.
• Cut four 10 x 7-inch rectangles for pockets and pocket linings.

Assembly

Use ¼-inch-wide seam allowances.

1. Stitch one pocket lining to each end of wrap front, right sides together (Figure 1).

Figure 1

2. Stitch remaining two pockets to wrap ends, right sides together (Figure 2).

Figure 2

3. With right sides together, stitch wrap ends to wrap front, leaving pockets free (Figure 3).

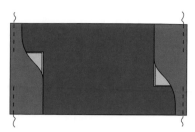

Figure 3

4. Pull pocket lining through opening and press well. Stitch sides of pockets (Figure 4).

Figure 4

5. With right sides together, stitch wrap front to wrap back, leaving a 6-inch opening on one side for turning (Figure 5). ***Note:*** *Be sure to catch bottom edges of pockets in stitching.*

Figure 5

6. Turn wrap right side out. Hand-stitch opening closed. ⏱

Pop Art Handkerchief Top

Design by Paula Smith-Danell

Sew this poncho-style cover-up top from a rectangle of chiffon fabric. You'll be so pleased with how fast and easy this top is to sew that you'll want to make this versatile top to coordinate all of your looks.

Estimated Time
2½ hours

Top

Finished size
One size fits most

Materials
- 45-inch-wide silk chiffon fabric:
    - 1¾ yards for body*
    - 1½ yards for contrast
- Silk pins
- French curve
- View-through ruler
- Basic sewing supplies and equipment

⅓ yard will be used for squaring edges and testing fabric.

Preparation
Test fabric's ability to tear along the grain line by making a clip in the selvage edge 1½ inches from the cut edge and at least 1 inch deep. Grasp both edges securely. Pull gently and see if the fabric will tear along the cross grain. Limited puckering can be pressed out using an iron set on medium heat with steam.

If fabric will not tear or there is excessive puckering or pulled threads, then square-cut the edge of the fabric by pulling a weft (cross-grain) thread.

Cutting

Tear or square-cut fabric as explained in Preparation.

From silk chiffon for body:

• Measure 50 inches along selvage edge and tear or square-cut so fabric measures 50 x 45 inches.

From contrasting silk chiffon:

• Tear or square-cut two 50 x 6-inch strips along the straight of grain (selvages).
• Fold remaining fabric on the bias. Pin and press fold. Use a view-through ruler to mark a 1 x 28-inch strip along the fold (Figure 1). Cut along marked line for bias binding.

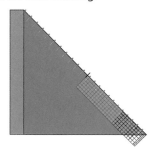

Figure 1

Assembly

***Note:** Refer to Assembly Diagram (page 17) throughout.*

1. Turn under and stitch a ½-inch hem on cut edges of body.

2. With wrong sides together, fold body piece in half, matching hemmed edges. Pin fold and press lightly for shoulder fold. Unfold, then fold again, matching selvage edges. Pin this fold and press lightly near center for center front/back fold.

Quick Tip

Pattern Option: For a quick variation, cut or tear fabric to 51 x 50 inches. Stitch a ½-inch hem on all sides and omit instructions for the contrast trim.

3. Using air- or water-soluble marking pen, mark center front fold 2 inches from pressed shoulder fold; mark center back fold ½ inch from shoulder fold (Figure 2).

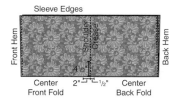

Figure 2

4. Mark shoulder fold 4½ inches from center front/back fold. Using a French curve, draw the neck curve for the front, connecting marks at center front and shoulder (Figure 3). Using a French curve, mark a line connecting the mark at the center back fold to the shoulder fold mark (Figure 4).

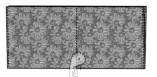

Figure 3

Figure 4

5. Cut out neck opening and mark center back fold line at the neck edge. Beginning at center back, with right sides together and raw edges even, pin bias binding around neck edge, leaving an extra 1 inch beyond center back mark at beginning and end for center back seam allowance.

6. With right sides together, stitch center back seam in binding (Figure 5). Trim excess. Press. Sew binding to neck edge using a ⅜-inch seam allowance. Clip seam allowance ⅛ inch deep at shoulder curves to ease binding into these areas.

Figure 5

7. Press seam allowance toward binding. Carefully trim excess allowance. Edge-stitch binding ⅛ inch from seam line, catching seam allowance. Turn binding inside neckline. Pin in place and press lightly from wrong side. Beginning at center back, with binding on top, topstitch ⅜ inch from neckline edge. Press.

8. Pin right side of each contrast strip to wrong side of body along one selvage edge, with edges even, allowing contrast strip to extend at least ½ inch on each end of body (Figure 6). Sew, using a ½-inch seam allowance. Press seam allowance toward body.

Figure 6

9. Press under ½ inch on remaining long edge of contrast strip. Fold strip with right sides together and stitch across ends so stitching lines are even with body hems (Figure 7). Turn and press. Pin contrast fabric over body seam allowance so edges of contrast fabric are even. Edge-stitch ⅛ inch from edge of fold (Figure 8).

Figure 7

Figure 8

10. Fold body with wrong sides together along shoulder seam. Measure 13½ inches from each end. Mark 13½-inch lines parallel with ends of garment. Stitch along line, securing beginning and ending of stitching. Remove basting threads. ⏱

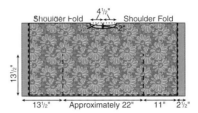

Handkerchief Top Assembly Diagram

Chiffon

Chiffon is a lightweight, sheer, plain-weave fabric with a dull finish. It has a soft hand and drapes well. It is made with fine, highly twisted yarns and has an even number of threads per inch in both the warp (longwise) and the weft (crosswise). Originally, chiffon was made of silk, but now can be found in rayon, polyester and other man-made filament fibers.

Tools: Use fine, sharp silk pins; sharp scissors or rotary cutter with mat; high-quality, extra-fine cotton-covered polyester thread; and fine sewing-machine needles sizes 60/8 or 65/9.

Cutting chiffon: Chiffon can be difficult to cut. Tearing the fabric along the grain line when using silk chiffon is best. Using extra fabric, check to see that fabric will tear without excessive puckering. Some synthetic-fiber chiffons will not tear, so pulling a thread to guide your cutting is recommended. Spraying chiffon with fabric starch is also a helpful aid in cutting.

Stole the Show Shawl

Design by Dorothy Martin

Make this luxurious featherweight shawl in just a few hours. Embellish it with sparkles or dashes of color to complete your beautiful evening ensemble. The graceful flowing ruffle is achieved without the bulk of gathering.

Estimated Time
2 hours

Shawl

Finished size
Approximately 53½ inches across top and 37½ inches on each side, excluding ruffle

Ruffle is approximately 2¾ inches wide

Materials
• 2 yards 60-inch-wide silk or polyester organza
• 6 yards ⅛-inch metallic braid
• Optional: hot-fix crystals and applicator
• Template plastic or card stock
• Basic sewing supplies and equipment

Cutting
Enlarge ruffle template (page 21) 200 percent. Use pattern to cut template from plastic or card stock. Cut through edge of template to inner circle and cut out inner circle as indicated on template.

• Cut a 38 x 38-inch square for shawl body.
• From remaining fabric, use template to cut nine pieces for ruffles on the straight grain of fabric.

Shawl Assembly
Use ¼-inch-wide seam allowances. ***Note:*** *This is included in ruffle template.*

1. Staystitch the four sides of the shawl body. Make a thread loop to hold shawl points together when wearing: Twist 12 (12-inch) lengths of thread together and machine-zigzag over them. (Figure 1).

Figure 1

Note: *Refer to Shawl Diagram throughout.*

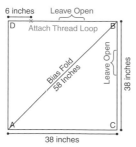

Shawl Diagram

2. At approximately 6 inches from one shawl corner, pin ends of thread loop to the right side of the body, to be included in the seam allowance.

3. Join cut edges of the short side of ruffle pieces to make one continuous length. Finish seam edges.

Quick Tips

For greater accuracy, calculate the exact amount of trim required by measuring the hemmed ruffle after it is stitched to the body.

If working with a limited amount of fabric, make a larger inner circle in the template. This will result in a longer ruffle that is less full and not as deep as the template provided.

Make samples of planned hem embellishment prior to final stitching on the shawl to be certain the embellishment has the desired effect.

Staystitch lines are particularly important in featherweight fabrics to maintain shape and provide a guideline for subsequent stitching.

There is no need to back-tack stitching lines that will later be overstitched. This decreases bulk in seam areas.

4. Staystitch the inner edge of the joined ruffle length as shown on the template. Clip the inner-circle edges to the staystitching line at ½-inch intervals. Staystitch ruffle outer edges.

5. With right sides together, pin inner edge of ruffle to two continuous edges of the shawl (sides AC and CB). At point C, take a small tuck in the ruffle to give fullness to the corner turn. Stitch, leaving the first and last 3 inches of ruffle free. **Note:** *Occasionally lift presser foot and adjust ruffle fabric as needed to avoid ripples in the stitching line.*

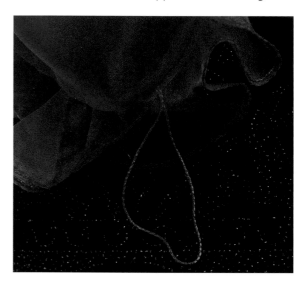

6. Using a narrow-hem presser foot, if available, hem ruffle edge with a narrow hem and multiple zigzag stitch. Stitch ⅛-inch-wide metallic braid to ruffle hem with zigzag stitch.

7. At the beginning and end of the ruffle, finish the short straight edge with a hem, or continue the hem embellishment into seam allowance. In the latter, the ruffle corner can be trimmed into a gentle curve.

8. Fold the shawl on the bias line, point D to point C. Pin the right sides together, enclosing the ruffle and working remaining 3 inches of ruffle into respective corners of shawl.

9. Designate a 9-inch area to be the pull-through length; overcast these seam allowances separately.

This area will be hand-tacked closed later. Stitch the shawl sides together (leaving the 9-inch area open) and overcast the seam with a zigzag stitch, except for the 9-inch opening.
Trim threads.

10. Gently pull shawl right side out, and hand-tack the opening closed. If desired, add hot-fix crystals randomly following manufacturer's instructions. ⟳

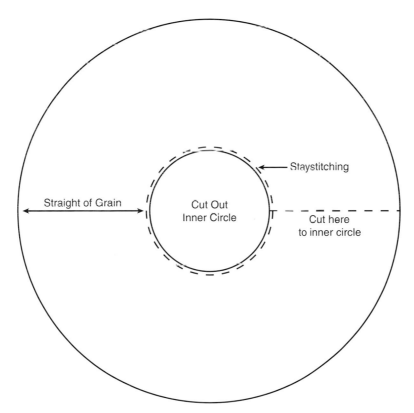

Stole the Show Shawl Ruffle Template
Enlarge 200%

Straight of Grain

Cut Out
Inner Circle

Staystitching

Cut here
to inner circle

Celebrate Denim Jacket

Design by Linda Turner Griepentrog

Flying the flag isn't limited to July 4th. It's an everyday right we cherish. Gather some red, white and blue fabrics and decorate your denim in spirit with a stylized stars-and-stripes appliqué collage!

Estimated Time
4 hours

Jacket

Finished size
Your size

Materials
- Purchased denim jacket
- 44/45-inch-wide cotton print fabric:
    ¼ yard red print for stripe, collar and cuff lining
    Scraps 2 red prints for stripe and stars
    Scraps 3 white prints for stripes and stars
    Scraps 4 blue prints for stripes and stars
- 8½ x 11-inch sheet ready-to-print fabric
- Paper-backed fusible web
- Optional: fusible interfacing
- Red, white and blue 10mm iron-on stars
- Hot-fix applicator tool
- Metallic machine-embroidery thread
- Basic sewing supplies and equipment

Project note: Depending on size and style of jacket, it may be necessary to resize stripes so they lay within jacket seams.

Preparation
1. Trace around collar and cuffs on pattern tracing paper, adding ¼ inch seam allowance all around.

2. On paper side of fusible web, use patterns (page 25) to trace three long stripes, three short stripes, two large stars, three medium stars and two small stars. Cut out slightly outside traced lines.

Cutting
If needed to prevent color show-through, fuse interfacing to wrong sides of fabrics before applying fusible web.

From red print for stripe, collar and cuff lining:
- Fuse one long stripe onto wrong side of fabric. Cut out on traced line.
- Use traced patterns to cut two cuffs and one collar.

From two red prints for stripes and stars:
- Fuse one short stripe onto wrong side of one fabric. Cut out on traced line.
- Fuse two large stars onto wrong side of second fabric. Cut out on traced lines.

From three white prints for stripes and stars:
• Fuse one long stripe and one short stripe onto wrong side of each of two fabrics. Cut out on traced lines.
• Fuse two medium stars onto wrong side of third fabric. Cut out on traced lines.

From four blue prints for stripes and stars:
• Fuse one long stripe and one short stripe onto wrong side of each of two fabrics. Cut out on traced lines.
• Fuse one medium and one small star onto wrong side of third fabric. Cut out on traced lines.
• Fuse one small star onto wrong side of fourth fabric. Cut out on traced lines.

Assembly

1. Referring to photo for placement, arrange stripes on back of jacket. Fuse in place following manufacturer's instructions. Arrange stars as shown and fuse in place.

2. Embellish stripes as desired with metallic embroidery thread and decorative stitching. Use a medium-width zigzag stitch to outline stripes.

3. Use hot-set applicator tool to randomly apply red, white and blue stars following manufacturer's instructions.

4. Print the word "Celebrate" onto ready-to-print fabric using a size 72–80-point font. Back the fabric with paper-backed fusible web and draw a rectangle around the lettering. Cut out and fuse to jacket below flag.

5. Outline lettering patch using medium-width zigzag stitch and contrasting thread. Add stars at corners.

6. Turn under ¼-inch seam allowances on collar and cuff linings. ***Note:*** *Cuffs will no longer snap since the fastener will be covered with fabric.* Hand-stitch linings around edges of cuffs and collar. ○

Sources: *Ready-to-Print fabric sheets from Jacquard Products; Iron-on stars and Kandi Kane hot-fix applicator tool from Kandi Corp.; metallic machine-embroidery thread from Sulky of America; Steam-A-Seam2 paper-backed fusible web from The Warm Company.*

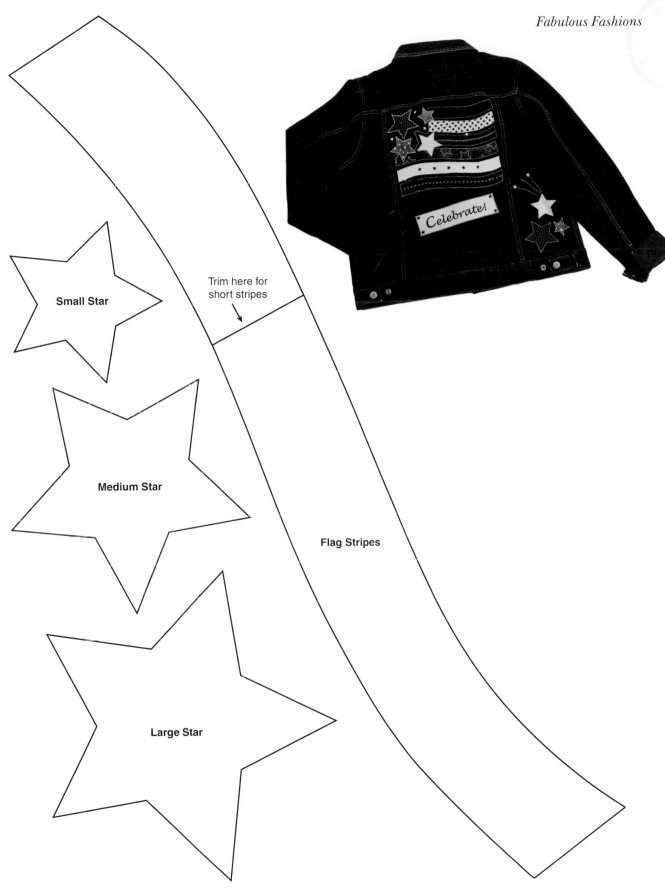

Small Star

Trim here for
short stripes

Medium Star

Flag Stripes

Large Star

Celebrate Denim Jacket Templates
Actual Size

Over-the-Top Denim

Design by Zoe Graul

Turn any front-closure denim shirt or dress into a new, funky top in an afternoon or less. You'll still have plenty of time left in the day to wear your new denim creation and be the envy of all your friends.

Estimated Time
3 hours

Shirt

Finished size
Your size

Materials
• Denim dress or shirt
• ¾ yard 44-inch-wide sheer fabric*
• 3 medium snap fasteners
• Optional: 3 decorative buttons
• Basic sewing supplies and equipment
*If front and back measurement is more than
 40 inches (see step 2), 1¼ yards are needed.*

Preparation
1. Determine desired length of denim bodice and cut off shirt or, if using an empire-waist dress, remove skirt from bodice. Remove stitching from placket facing 1 inch from cut edge (Figure 1).

Figure 1

2. With front opening closed, use pins to mark center front and center back of shirt at bottom edge. Measure shirt as follows, adding 1 inch to each measurement:

Top Layers (measurement A): Measure around the shirt from center front to center back (Figure 2).

Figure 2

Back Bottom Layer (measurement B): Measure from side seam to side seam across the back (Figure 3).

Figure 3

Front Bottom Layer (measurement C): Measure from side seam to side seam across the front (Figure 4).

Figure 4

3. Try on the top. Measure from the bottom of the bodice to the desired length of the completed shirt. Add 1 inch to this measurement for bottom hem and seam allowance.

4. Fold fabric lengthwise in half, matching selvages. ***Note:*** *Use selvage edges for center back and sides if needed.* For bottom front layer, cut one piece the desired length by the bottom front measurement (C).

5. For bottom back layer, cut one piece the desired length by the bottom back measurement (B).

6. For top layers, cut two pieces the width of the top layers measurement (A) and 2–4 inches shorter than the bottom layers.

7. Serge or zigzag raw edges to prevent fraying. Fold a ¼-inch double-fold hem on sides; press and stitch hems. Repeat on bottom edges.

Use extra sheer fabric to make a scarf that can double as a belt.

Before pinning on the top layers, add fringe trim to the bodice at the seam.

If extra fullness is desired at the hips, make the layers wider and gather them slightly at the top before stitching them to the bodice.

Assembly

Use ½-inch-wide seam allowances, unless otherwise noted.

1. With right sides together and raw edges even, pin top layers to bodice from center front to center back. Stitch around bodice using a longer stitch than normal (Figure 5). ***Note:*** *Pin up placket facing to avoid catching it in the stitching.*

Figure 5

2. Pin the back bottom layer to the back of the bodice over the top layers, matching centers. Stitch.

3. Pin center of front bottom layer to center front of bodice at edge of placket. Press and stitch a ¼-inch double-fold hem in right front top edge of front bottom layer. ***Note:*** *Front bottom layer is stitched to bodice on left side only.* Pin remaining unfinished edge to left front bodice from center to side seam. Stitch.

4. Press seam allowances toward denim bodice and pin. Remove pin from placket facing. Turn under edges of placket and facing; hand-stitch in place.

5. Using thread to match topstitching on denim, topstitch close to folded edge of bodice and again ¼ inch from first stitching. Stitch over placket where stitching was removed.

6. Sew one snap at the bottom of the placket and one to secure the bottom layer to the right side seam. Sew a third snap centered between the previous two.

7. If desired, remove shirt buttons and replace with decorative buttons.

8. Follow care instructions for sheer fabric when laundering. ⏱

Update Your Denim Skirt

Design by Chris Malone

This is a great project for busy weekend afternoons when you know you'll spend time sitting and waiting or riding in a car. Pre-mark the embroidery design on your skirt, stuff your sewing basket with supplies and stitch to your heart's content.

Estimated Time
5 hours

Skirt

Finished size
Your size

Materials
- Denim skirt, mid-calf length, fairly straight
- Pearl cotton size 5:
    - orange #946
    - red #321
    - rust #920
    - yellow #725
    - blue #807
    - green #3347
- Optional: 13 (⁹⁄₁₆-inch) green buttons
- Glass E beads:
    - 14 yellow
    - 3 blue
- Embroidery needle
- Embroidery hoop
- Basic sewing supplies and equipment

Project note: *Study your skirt to determine the most flattering arrangement for embroidery motifs. Referring to photo and templates for placement, position flowers first, and then add stems, tendrils and leaves, altering placement as necessary for the most flattering fit.*

Pattern Transfer

There are different methods of transferring patterns:

Cut out patterns and draw around them.

If material is light in weight and color, use a light box or a bright window and trace the design.

For more intricate patterns, use dressmaker's carbon and a stylus, sharp pencil or tracing wheel.

Instructions

Refer to stitch illustrations on page 33.

1. Chain-stitch around each flower center with blue pearl cotton. In the center of the upper left (red) flower only, chain-stitch another line inside the first.

2. Chain-stitch all inner petals with yellow pearl cotton. Chain-stitch outer petals, using orange on right flower, red on upper left flower and rust on lower left flower.

3. Use green and outline or stem stitch to stitch leaves, tendrils and stems. Use fly stitch to stitch veins in each leaf.

4. Add a green button at the end of each tendril, if desired, stitching with green pearl cotton.

5. Use a doubled strand of matching thread to sew three blue beads in the center of the red flower and seven yellow beads in the centers of the remaining two flowers.

6. Sew five green buttons on each pocket flap (if applicable) with green pearl cotton. ⏲

Sources: *Pearl cotton from DMC.*

Pressing & Embellishing Tips

When embellishing clothing with embroidery, buttons and beads, it is very important that the work be as secure as possible.

Use a sturdy knot and avoid long stitches on the front and back that can easily snag. A tiny drop of seam sealant or fabric glue applied to each knot will add extra strength.

Attach beads with two stitches and doubled thread and make a knot after every one or two beads so if the thread should catch on something and break, you will not lose all the beads.

To press a garment that has dimensional stitching and embellishments, place the item right side down on a terry cloth towel and press from the back. The texture of the towel will protect the embellishments from the heat and keep the stitches from being flattened.

Chain Stitch

Fly Stitch

Outline Stitch

Upper Left Flower

Right Flower

Update Your Denim Skirt Templates
Enlarge 200%

Lower Left Flower

Autumn Print
T-Shirt

Designs by Missy Shepler

We've captured autumn leaves, photographed them and printed the designs to fabric, but the sky is the limit with this project.

Estimated Time
3 hours

T-Shirt

Finished size
Your size

Materials
- Purchased cotton T-shirt
- Selection of autumn leaves
- Printable cotton poplin fabric sheets
- Home computer with ink-jet printer and image-editing program
- Basic sewing supplies and equipment

Instructions

1. Use computer to print leaves onto ready-to-print fabric.

2. Carefully cut around printed leaf, leaving a slight border. **Option:** *Box the image or cut a simplified shape that will be easier to stitch.*

3. Lightly spray back of printed image with temporary adhesive and position on front of shirt. Zigzag-stitch around edges of image.

4. Pull threads to inside. Clip threads and apply seam sealant to ends. Press with a dry iron. ◷

Gathering Images

Many companies offer photographs and clip art collections on CD or downloadable from Web sites. If you own a digital camera or scanner, you can easily click and create original art from found objects or personal photographs. The only limit is your own imagination!

Note: Be sure to abide by copyright laws that may apply to images that you don't create yourself.

Other Applications

Don't limit yourself to just T-shirts with this technique. Try these fun to make projects:

Instead of hand appliquéing "cherish" found on Cherish the Moment Journal cover (page 110), use the leaf appliqué instead.

Try appliquéd leaves on the Glowing Sweatshirt Redo, page 50. Instead of the fabric panel, try appliquéing leaves or cut the panel from coordinating fabric and appliqué on top of the panel and sweatshirt fabric.

Stitching Tips

Adjust the stitch setting so it is wide enough to cover the unprinted fabric edge and extend slightly into the T-shirt fabric.

Heavier thread creates a fuller stitched edge.

Use a ball point needle on knits. It will penetrate the fabric easier and cause less distortion of the knit fabric during appliqué.

Take care not to stretch knit fabric. It may be helpful to use a fabric stabilizer on stretchy fabrics.

Stop stitching as necessary, place the needle in a down position, raise the presser foot and pivot the fabric to stitch around leaf being careful not to stretch the knit fabric.

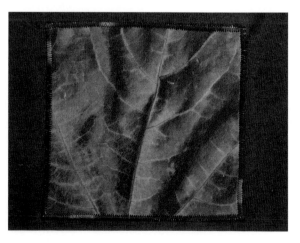

Printing

Printing Tips

Test print on paper. Check image size, placement and color. If printing multiple images on a single page, make sure there is adequate room for seam allowances all the way around.

Check ink levels in printer cartridges, or consider installing fresh cartridges if you will be doing a lot of fabric printing. Partially used cartridges can be stored in air-tight plastic bags and re-inserted later.

Fabric tends to absorb more ink than paper. Select the best print setting and increase the saturation and ink volume if these options are available in the print dialog box of the software program you are using.

Fabric tends to be thicker or heavier than standard printing paper. If necessary, choose a heavy or thick paper print option, usually found under paper type or quality. You may need to use a manual-feed setting.

Clip, don't pull, loose threads from fabric edge. Make sure there are no errant threads or clippings left on fabric—these will act as a resist, creating blank spots on the print.

Don't despair over misfeeds or misprints. You may be able to use a portion of the print or create a unique image by reprinting another image over the top of the misprint.

Remove all paper from the printer paper tray and insert ready-to-print fabric sheets one at a time.

Be patient. It can take time to learn what works best with your particular printer.

Get It Printed

If you can print on paper, you can print on fabric.

Use a home computer and ink-jet printer to print digital images onto ready-to-print fabric. All-in-one machines offer scanning and camera-card reading options in addition to printing capabilities.

Depending on your image source, you may need to make some adjustments to your image before printing. An image-editing program, such as Adobe Photoshop, is an excellent software tool for making image adjustments and, if desired, applying special effects to an image.

Many companies offer a variety of ready-to-print fabrics. Fabric options include white- or cream-colored cotton, linen or silk in a variety of weights and weaves. Choose a fabric type and weight that will work well with your purchased garment.

To print on fabric, take the same steps as printing on paper: Open the image you wish to print in the software program of your choice, make desired adjustments and print.

Follow manufacturer's instructions for post-printing fabric treatments. Many companies recommend a specific amount of drying time. Peel paper backing from printed fabric, taking care not to distort fabric. Some products require rinsing the printed image to remove excess ink, while others require heat-setting with a dry iron. Avoid using steam, which may cause water spots on freshly printed images.

At-the-Knee Jeans

Design by Sheila Zent

Restyle your old jeans into updated capris with a patched-denim border around each shortened hem. This technique has a hidden benefit—no bulky layers of denim to sew over.

Estimated Time
2 hours

Jeans

Finished size
Your size

Materials
- 1 pair denim jeans
- Scraps various shades faded denim
- Basic sewing supplies and equipment

Cutting
- Try on jeans and mark the bottom of each knee. Take jeans off. Mark a cut line 2½ inches below the knee mark on each leg. *Note: Measure the inner and outer seams on each leg to make sure length is equal on both sides* (Figure 1).

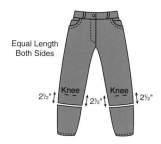

Figure 1

- From trimmed pant legs and denim scraps, cut matching pairs of strips each 3 x 6 inches. *Note: Make sure strips are cut on grain with each long edge following a single vertical thread. Depending on the width of the pant legs, you will need seven, eight or nine pairs of strips.*

Assembly

1. Remove stitches on outer seam from bottom edge of pant leg to the knee mark. Open seam allowance; clip as needed. Topstitch around slit on each leg (Figure 2).

Figure 2

2. On each denim strip, draw a line ½ inch from one long edge. Lap one strip over a contrasting strip, using the line as a guide for matching edges. Stitch strips together through the center of the overlap (Figure 3).

Figure 3

3. Continue joining strips in a random arrangement of different shades until the patchwork border contains one strip from each pair of strips (Figure 4).

Figure 4

4. Join remaining strips in same manner to make two matching borders. On the right side of each border, unravel a few long threads so the long edges appear slightly fringed, but not too close to the stitching.

5. Fold borders in half lengthwise and press a crease along the fold. Unfold the borders. With right sides together, pin one border to the bottom of one pant leg. Allowing the border to extend slightly at each end for fringing, trim excess length to fit. Stitch, using ½-inch seam allowance. Attach remaining border to opposite leg in mirror-image arrangement.

6. Press seam allowances toward border. Zigzag or serge opposite edge of each border. Refold border on crease so serged edge is inside pant leg. Stitch in the ditch to secure inside border edge. Topstitch open ends closed (Figure 5).

Figure 5

7. Machine-wash and dry to fluff up raw edges. Trim threads, seam allowances or edges as desired. ⏱

Top Off
Your T-Shirt

Design by Lynn Weglarz

To create a fast and easy designer touch to your plain-Jane T-shirt, insert godets at the sleeve hems and add a strip of the same fabric to the neckline. Instant pizzazz!

Estimated Time
1 ½ hours

T-Shirt

Finished Size
Your size

Materials
• Long-sleeve T-shirt with V-shaped neckline
• ¼ yard stretch lace or chiffon to match T-shirt
• Basic sewing supplies and equipment

Cutting
From stretch lace or chiffon:
• Use godet template to cut six pieces.
• Cut a 1–2-inch strip the width of the fabric for neckline.

Assembly
Use scant ¼-inch-wide seam allowances unless otherwise stated.

***Note:** If using chiffon, use a rolled edge finish on one long edge of the neckline strip and bottom edge of each godet with woolly nylon in upper looper before inserting in T-shirt.*

1. Beginning at bottom of V-shaped neckline, pin one long edge of strip to inside of neckline edge along seam line, overlapping ends slightly. Trim off excess. Topstitch strip in place.

2. Measure 7 inches up from sleeve hem and chalk a line around sleeve (Figure 1).

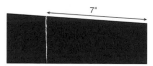

Figure 1

3. Measure 1 inch from sleeve seam toward the front of the T-shirt and chalk a line up to the 7-inch chalk line (Figure 2). Cut along this line.

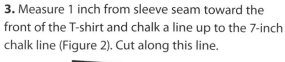

Figure 2

4. With right sides together, pin the godet to one side of the cut edge (Figure 3). Stitch from godet point to outside edge. Repeat to stitch the other side of the godet to the cut edge of the sleeve (Figure 4).

Figure 3   **Figure 4**

5. Measure 1 inch from the sleeve seam toward the back of the T-shirt and chalk a line up to the 7-inch line. Cut along this line. Pin and stitch the second godet.

6. The third godet will be roughly 4 inches from the sleeve seam (or what would be the middle of the sleeve). Measure up to the 7-inch line; cut, pin and stitch the third godet. Repeat steps 2–6 for second sleeve. ⏱

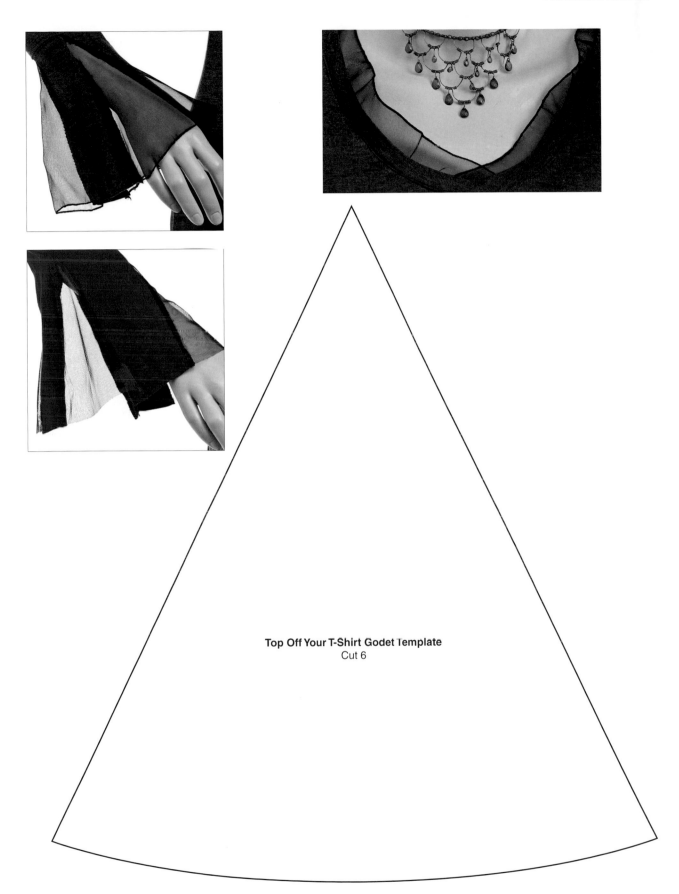

Top Off Your T-Shirt Godet Template
Cut 6

Fuzzy Fleecy Fun Neckwear

Design by Lynn Weglarz

This unique scarf has an easy way of ventilation. Too warm? Unzip your scarf. Or zip up to warm up. The diagonal design will keep the zipper away from your face and chin.

Estimated Time
1½ hours

Scarf

Finished size
21 inches in circumference by 8 inches tall

Materials
• ¼ yard outerwear fleece
• ⅛ yard swimwear fabric for binding
• 1 (9-inch) outerwear zipper with closed bottom
• Basic sewing supplies and equipment

Cutting
From outerwear fleece:
• Cut two 27 x 8-inch rectangles. Mark wrong sides of rectangles. With right sides together, cut ends as shown in diagram (Figure 1).

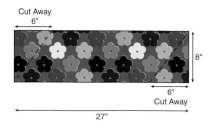

Cut Away
6"

8"

6"
Cut Away

27"

Figure 1

From swimwear fabric:
• Cut two 21 x 2-inch strips (with the greatest stretch along the 21-inch edge) for binding.

Assembly
Use scant ¼-inch-wide seam allowances unless otherwise stated. Sew right sides together.

1. With fleece layered right sides together, sandwich zipper between layers along one angled edge. Pin and stitch.

2. Stitch remaining edge of zipper to opposite edge of fleece in same manner. ***Note:*** *Scarf will be twisted and look wrong.*

Turn scarf right side out and flatten layers together. Trim top and bottom edges even.

3. Sew short edges of one swimwear binding strip together. Pin binding to fleece with raw edges even; stitch.

4. Fold binding over edges of fleece and pin in place. Stitch in the ditch to secure binding on inside of scarf. Trim binding close to stitching line.

5. Sew remaining swimwear binding strip to top edge of fleece in same manner, turning under ends at zipper opening. ⏱

Quick Tips

Mark fleece quickly and easily with a piece of low-tack tape; remove tape after stitching.

Try using corduroy, in great color and wale variations, or knit suede to bind the scarf. Allow an extra ¼ yard of fabric for the corduroy and cut it on the bias. Knit suede also comes in many different colors and can be cut on the crosswise grain (with the greatest stretch) rather than on the bias, so extra fabric is not required.

Standing Room Only Stadium Jacket

Design by Bev Shenefield

Sew this fun fringed jacket made from two stadium fringed blankets in an afternoon and wear it to cheer your favorite team to victory.

Estimated Time
3 hours

Jacket

Finished size
One size fits most

Materials
- 2 (50 x 60-inch) stadium blankets with fringe
- 1 toggle fastener
- Basic sewing supplies and equipment

Cutting
- Referring to diagrams (Figures 1 and 2 on page 48) lay out blankets with right sides up and cut one body, two sleeves, one collar, two 27-inch lengths of fringe and two 4½-inch lengths of fringe.

- Make a 13-inch slit 12½ inches from each side of body (Figure 1) for sleeve openings.

Assembly
Use ½-inch-wide seam allowances unless otherwise stated.

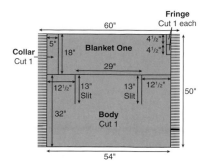

Figure 1

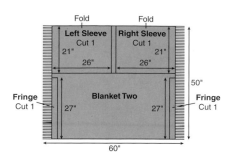

Figure 2

1. With wrong sides of sleeves facing up, turn under raw edges opposite fringe. Bring folded edge of each sleeve to fringe edge and topstitch close to folded edge through all thicknesses.

2. Fold body at sleeve slits, right sides together. For shoulder seams, sew across top edges of body from each sleeve slit to 3½ inches from the front fringe.

3. Sew sleeves in slit openings, matching seams.

4. With right sides together and raw edges even, sew 4½-inch lengths of fringe to ends of collar. Fold seam allowances to wrong side of collar and whipstitch to collar.

5. With right side of collar and wrong side of body together and raw edges even, sew collar to body, matching fringe on collar with fringe on body. Fold collar back.

6. Turn sleeves up desired hem length and hand-stitch. Trim away fringe inside sleeves.

7. Sew two 27-inch lengths of fringe together. Sew bottom selvage edge of body over edge of fringe.

8. Sew toggle fastener to jacket front approximately 15 inches from neckline. ⏱

Glowing Sweatshirt Redo

Design by Susan Breier

Create this simple sweatshirt redo from fabric odds and ends, notions and embellishments in hours. By using a ready-to-wear top, most of the garment sewing is done for you, leaving plenty of time for you to express your creativity.

Estimated Time
4 hours

Sweatshirt

Finished size
Your size

Materials
- Cotton or cotton-blend sweatshirt with set-in sleeves
- Cotton fabric for embellishment areas (approximately ¾ yard) for the accent panel*
- Lightweight fusible web
- Fabric stabilizer
- 1 (3-yard) package ⅞-inch-wide single-fold bias tape
- Buttons or beads in 2 or more sizes
- ⅞-inch button for closure
- 6 inches colored cord for button loop
- 1-inch-wide masking or painter's tape
- Fabric glue
- Basic sewing supplies and equipment

The panel width for model project is 6 inches on a women's large shirt.

Project notes: *Choose a sweatshirt that has set-in sleeves and fits slightly large. The correct arm length is important.*
Machine-wash and dry sweatshirt and embellishment fabric. Do not use fabric softener.

Sweatshirt Front

1. Place sweatshirt on a flat surface with the front side up. Cut the bottom ribbing off evenly. **Note:** *Do not remove the collar or cuff ribbing.*

2. Mark a 24-inch line down the center front (Figure 1). Place 1-inch-wide masking tape on each side of the line, allowing ⅛ inch between the two pieces (Figure 2 on page 52). **Note:** *This will stop any rolling or stretching and serve as a marker for your front embellishments.*

24"

Figure 1

⅞"

Figure 2

3. With the shirt lying flat, cut the center front from the bottom up through the collar area between the tape markers. **Note:** *Side vents will be cut later.*

4. Determine width of accent panel and cut from cotton fabric. **Note:** *Panel is positioned at least 1¼ inches from the center taped area of the sweatshirt.* Following manufacturer's instructions, apply lightweight fusible web to wrong side of panel fabric, covering an area slightly larger than desired size of finished panel on top, bottom and inside edges and avoiding approximately 2 inches of the panel area on the outer edge of the panel (to reduce stiffness).

5. Cut accent panel 2 inches longer at the top and 2 inches longer at the bottom than needed. Cut the sides on the exact design lines wanted.

Sleeve Adjustment

To correct too much bulk or length in the sleeves, turn the garment inside out. Beginning just above the elbow area, sew a new seam next to the original seam. When width of sleeve is reduced to desired size, trim off the excess fabric and zigzag the raw edges.

To shorten the sleeve, cut off the ribbing and press and stitch a 1-inch hem using the three rows of stitching as on the bottom hem.

6. Remove the paper backing from the fusible web. Pin the accent panel a minimum of 1¼ inches from the center taped area. Try on the garment and make adjustments as needed. Fuse panel to the right side of the garment with 2 inches extending beyond the shoulder seam. **Note:** *Avoid pressing the 1-inch-wide tape.*

7. Use the ribbed neckline as a guide for shaping the top of the panel. Lightly mark the face of the panel around the lower edge of the neckline rib to determine the cutting line. Apply extra fusible web under the cutting line at the collar edge. Press the panel around the bottom of the collar and carefully trim off the excess fabric. When cool, open the right shoulder seam with a seam ripper enough to allow the top of the accent panel to slide through and be hidden. Press the shoulder seam area. Turn the garment to the wrong side. Trim off the excess panel fabric and stitch the shoulder seam closed.

8. Trim the bottom edge of the accent panel so it ends at the bottom of the sweatshirt. Pin stabilizer under the sweatshirt in the accent panel area. **Note:** *This will help the fabric to move evenly under the presser foot and attain uniform stitching. Shorter-than-normal stitches weaken the stabilizer or tissue product for easier removal.* Use a straight stitch to stitch the accent panel to the sweatshirt following distinct pattern lines on the fabric panel. A blanket or zigzag stitch works well on the outer edges of the panel and around the panel at the neck band. Remove the stabilizer after the panel is secured.

9. Carefully remove the lengths of tape to prevent distortion of the fabric. Cut two lengths of ⅞-inch-wide bias tape at least 2 inches longer than the length of center front. Open the bias tape. Starting at the collar edge, fold bias tape end under ¼ inch at the top to cover the raw edge of the collar. With right sides together, match the raw unfolded edge of the bias tape with the raw edge of center front. Starting at the collar area, straight-stitch the entire length, following the fold line in the bias tape. At the bottom, trim excess bias tape and fold under ¼ inch.

10. Turn the free portion of the bias tape over to the wrong side of the garment. With the ¼-inch ends folded under, straight-stitch the unattached areas to the garment from the wrong side. Repeat for the other center front.

11. Try on your garment, pinning the center 1-inch panels so they overlap. Pin at the neck edge and in various areas along the front, making sure that the bottom hems match. Plan a 1½ x 2¼-inch design area just above the bustline, referring to photo for placement. Apply fusible web to fabric, and cut one or more pieces for this design as you did for the front panel. Pin pieces in place, adjust, and then permanently fuse in place. Stitch in same manner as front panel.

12. Hand-sew a ⅞-inch button onto the area, sewing through a snippet of bias tape on the inside of the garment for extra stability.

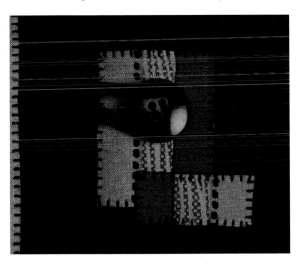

13. Cut a length of ⅛-inch cord to loop around the button with an additional section to slide into a reopened area of the right panel. Put the garment on and see if the jacket hangs straight and that the loop is in the correct position with the button. Open a ½-inch area on the right panel's outer row of stitching so the cord can be inserted, and then re-stitch that area to secure the loop ends. ***Note:***

You may wish to sew a small snap at the looped area for extra security and to help keep the bottom edge of the garment matching.

14. Fuse and cut a piece of panel fabric for back panel embellishment. This embellishment on the model project measures 5 x 1 inch. Fuse in place, centered on the back 1 inch from the ribbing of the collar. Stitch in same manner as panels on the front.

15. Hand-stitch small beads and or buttons to panels for added interest. Refer to Side Vents on page 54 before finishing the hem. If you chose to skip the side vents, continue with step 16.

Construction Hints

Never stretch the garment when sewing.

Avoid touching the 1-inch-wide masking tape with your iron.

Try the sweatshirt on several times throughout the project to evaluate the fit.

Use a needle-down position for accurate stitching.

A stiletto helps to guide the fabric evenly.

Hand-stitch beads or buttons to enhance the front and back panels.

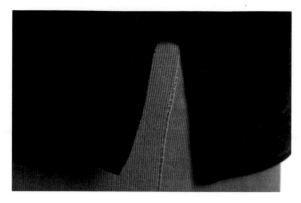

16. Finish bottom raw edge of sweatshirt/panel using edgestitch or zigzag stitch. Press a 1-inch hem to the wrong side of the garment using a press cloth, finger-pressing the taped front areas.

17. Plan to sew the hem of the sweatshirt in three separate sections (back, right front, left front) from the wrong side so you can easily view the raw edges as you sew. Using a stiletto to guide the fabric, carefully stitch the back hem to the back of the jacket at the bottom edge. Next, stitch ⅛ inch from the top raw edge of the hem. Stitch a second line ⅛ inch from the last top row. Repeat for the left front hem. When stitching the right front hem, avoid stitching through the panel. Secure that area with hand stitching and vertical stitches through the panel and sweatshirt fabric. ◷

Side Vents

Try on the shirt to determine if you need to alter the hip area with the use of side vents. If bottom is snug, add side vents as follows:

1. Place tape on each side of a 3½-inch line at each bottom side (Figure 3) as you did for the center front. Snip into top of each line ¼ inch to form a "Y."

Figure 3

2. Cut an 18-inch length of ⅞-inch-wide bias tape. Fold in half and press to make a narrow length of bias tape.

3. Carefully remove the masking tape on the garment to prevent stretching. Press ¼ inch of the shirt fabric to the inside. Adjust and pin two lengths of bias tape to cover the vertical raw edges of one vent. Add a small piece to cover the top raw edge (Figure 4). Use fabric glue and pins to hold in place.

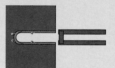

Figure 4

4. Sewing from the wrong side, using your needle down position and a stiletto, stitch in place. Repeat with a second row of stitches to secure all of the edges. Complete the other side vent.

Glorious Gifts

What better way to show how much you care than to give friends and loved ones a handcrafted gift. With the ideas in this chapter, you'll be able to handcraft a gift quickly and easily, and perhaps most importantly, create a one-of-a-kind designer gift that is sure to show your thoughtfulness.

It's All Black & White

Design by Linda Turner Griepentrog

Mixing fabric patterns adds fun and interest to any project. Try your skills on this simple pieced tote—only small swatches are needed to create an eclectic look.

Estimated Time
4 hours

Tote

Finished size
10 x 10 x 3 inches,
excluding handles

Materials
- 44/45-inch-wide quilting cotton fabric:
  - ¼ yard each 2 coordinating dark black-and-white prints
  - ½ yard 3rd coordinating dark black-and-white print
  - ¼ yard each 2 coordinating light black-and-white prints
- ½ yard 45-inch-wide canvas or stiff interfacing
- ½ yard lightweight cotton batting
- Paper-backed fusible web
- 1⅞-inch button form to cover
- 2 (6½-inch-long) black plastic oval purse handles
- 3½-inch silk flower
- 1½-inch pin back
- Fabric/craft glue
- Basic sewing supplies and equipment

Cutting

From first two dark black-and-white prints:
- Cut two 8¼ x 8¼-inch squares each.

From two light black-and-white prints:
- Cut two 8¼ x 8¼-inch squares each.

From third dark black-and-white print:
- Cut two 4 x 4½-inch rectangles for purse handle attachments.
- Cut two 17 x 16-inch rectangles for lining.

From canvas:
- Cut two 16 x 16-inch squares.

From fusible web:
- Cut two 16 x 16-inch squares.
- Cut two 4 x ½-inch strips.

From batting:
- Cut two 16 x 16-inch squares.

Piecing

Use ¼-inch-wide seam allowances.

1. Sew black-and-white 8¼-inch squares together in pairs with one light and one dark square in each pair.

2. Sew pairs together to make two four-square pieces for front and back of tote (Figure 1). ***Note:*** *The tote front and back may have different design-placement patterning.*

Figure 1

Assembly

1. Following manufacturer's instructions, apply fusible web squares to canvas squares. Remove paper backing and fuse batting to canvas.

2. Spray batting squares with temporary spray adhesive. Adhere pieced fabrics to batting squares.

3. Enlarge tote body template (page 59). Pin template onto each layered pieced fabric, matching seams with center placement lines on template. Cut out tote body pieces. Cut out bottom notches on each piece.

4. With right sides together, sew side and bottom seams of tote (Figure 2).

Figure 2

5. To box bottom corners, fold tote side seams to match center seam and stitch (Figure 3).

Figure 3

6. To make handle attachments, fold under ½ inch on short edges of each 4 x 4½-inch rectangle. Insert strips of fusible web under folded-under edges and fuse in place. Slip each attachment through handle and baste raw edges with wrong sides together.

7. With raw edges even, center handle attachments at tote upper edges and baste in place (Figure 4). ***Note:*** *Some purse handles have a right side that is rounded or beveled along the edge and a flat underside.*

Figure 4

8. Sew lining fabric together as for tote, leaving at least 6 inches of center bottom seam open for turning.

9. Slip tote inside lining so right side of tote and right side of lining are together and top raw edges are even, with handles sandwiched between. Sew upper edges together. ***Note:*** *Depending on the thickness of the handles, it may be necessary to use a zipper foot.*

10. Turn lining up over tote and hand- or machine-stitch opening closed. Push lining inside tote and press upper edges, rolling lining over the seam allowance. Stitch-in-the-ditch of the lining/tote seam.

11. Remove silk flower petals from stem and discard the dimensional center and any hard portions. Hand-stitch petal layers together at the center.

12. Remove wire shank from button form to create a flat back; cover the button with a scrap of coordinating fabric. Glue button to flower center. Glue pin back on back of flower. Let dry. Pin flower at pieced intersection on bag front. ⏱

Sources: Steam A Seam2 paper-backed fusible web and Warm & White batting from The Warm Company; Fabri-Tac permanent adhesive from Beacon Adhesives.

Patterned Fabrics

Vary the scale of the prints. While similar-size prints combine well, there's nothing to intrigue the eye, and the overall look can be ho-hum.

Consider positive/negative combinations of the same print. Black-with-white-dot fabric is great mixed with white-with-black-dot fabric.

Some fabrics provide instant mixing opportunities within themselves. In woven patterns, both sides can be the right side and are sometimes different in appearance, depending on the weave structure. Wide-patterned stripes offer the opportunity to cut and piece within the same fabric, as do border-print designs.

Try combining patterns that have at least one commonality: color, pattern shape or background. Mixing bold geometrics and gentle curves can look jarring.

The same print in different sizes is always a winning combination.

If you're doubtful about your skills in combining fabrics, let the fabric companies help. Most companies make coordinates within a fabric line, perfect for swatching into your sewn project.

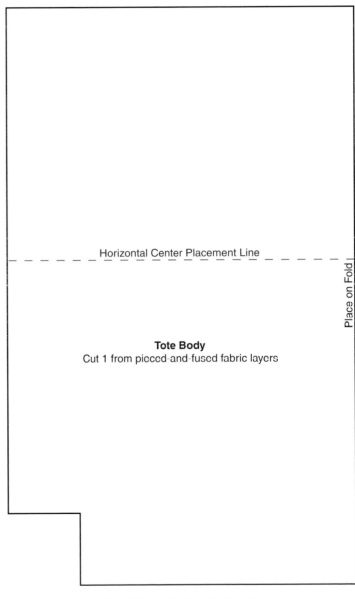

Horizontal Center Placement Line

Place on Fold

Tote Body
Cut 1 from pieced-and-fused fabric layers

It's All Black & White Template
Enlarge 200%

On the Go Laptop Cover

Design by Janis Bullis

Both professional and pretty, use this cover to carry your laptop or any important papers. Quilted with a thin layer of batting, it will gently protect your valuables. An outside pocket allows easy access to laptop accessories or personal items. This is a great gift to give or to keep for yourself.

Estimated Time
4 hours

Laptop Cover

Finished size
15 x 12 x 3 inches

Materials
- Mediumweight 44/45-inch-wide quilting fabric:
    - 1⅜ yards small print for outside
    - 1 yard solid or subtle print for piping and lining
- ½ yard cotton batting
- 24-inch plastic sport zipper
- 3 yards ⅜-inch decorator's filler cord
- Right-angle ruler
- Basic sewing supplies and equipment

Cutting
From small print fabric for outside:
- Cut one 16 x 29-inch rectangle for body. Using a small saucer as a template, round off corners.
- Cut one 10 x 10-inch rectangle for pocket.
- Cut two 4 x 28-inch boxing strips.
- Cut two 4 x 12-inch rectangles for ends.
- Cut two 3 x 46-inch strips for handles.

From fabric for piping and lining:
- Cut one 16 x 29-inch rectangle for body lining. Using a small saucer as a template, round off corners.
- Cut one 10 x 10-inch rectangle for pocket lining.
- Cut two 4 x 12-inch rectangles for end linings.
- Cut six 2 x 18-inch bias strips for piping.

From batting:
- Cut one 16 x 29-inch rectangle for body. Using a small saucer as a template, round off corners.
- Cut one 10 x 10-inch rectangle for pocket.
- Cut two 2 x 28-inch boxing strips.
- Cut two 4 x 12-inch rectangles for end batting.
- Cut two 1½ x 46-inch strips for handles.

Assembly

Use ½-inch-wide seam allowances unless otherwise stated.

Body & Pocket

1. On right side of body, locate center by folding fabric into quarters; mark center and unfold. With a right-angle ruler and air- or water-soluble fabric pen, draw parallel 45-degree-angle lines 2 inches apart across body in both directions (Figures 1 and 2).

Figure 1   **Figure 2**

2. Layer fabric with wrong sides together. Position batting between layers. Top stitch through fabric layers using 45-degree-angle lines as guides. **Note:** *If the fabric layers are shifting, use your walking foot on your sewing machine.*

3. Join short edges of bias strips together to make one long continuous strip. Cover filler cord and stitch close to cord using zipper foot to make covered piping. Cut a blunt end through cord and stitched fabric.

4. Beginning with the blunt end at the center of one long edge of the body, pin piping to the right side of the body with raw edges even. Stitch with your zipper foot, leaving 3 inches unstitched at the beginning and the end.

5. Remove 2 inches of stitching in the tail of the piping to expose the cord. Cut the tail of the end cord so it meets bluntly with the beginning cord. Tuck under the raw end of the piping fabric and wrap it around the cord, covering both ends.

Complete stitching the covered cord to the body. **Note:** *Reserve remaining piping for use on the pocket.*

6. Beginning at center of pocket, mark vertical lines on right side 1½ inches apart. Layer pocket batting on wrong side of pocket print. Stitch through fabric and batting on marked lines. Cut remaining piping 10 inches long. With raw edges even, pin and baste piping to right side of pocket top edge.

7. With pocket lining and pocket/batting right sides together, stitch across top edge close to piping cord with your zipper foot. Turn pocket to right side. Baste remaining three edges of pocket. Fold bottom edge of pocket under ½ inch.

8. Center pocket on right side of body 4 inches from top edge. Edgestitch sides and bottom of pocket to the body.

Handles & Boxing Strip

1. Pin each strip of handle batting to the wrong side of each fabric handle with one long edge of each even. Baste all edges of batting to fabric. With right sides together, baste long edges of fabric together, leaving a large opening for turning at center (Figure 3).

Figure 3

2. Turn each handle to the right side through the opening. Slip-stitch opening closed and press handle flat. Measure 11 inches in each direction from the center of the handle. Topstitch both edges of handle in this 22-inch center section (Figure 4).

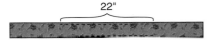

Figure 4

3. Stitch ends of handles together making one continuous loop. Pin handle seams at center of body 10 inches apart, parallel and covering pocket edges. Topstitch handles to body, beginning and ending at previous topstitching (Figure 5).

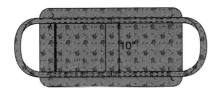

Figure 5

4. Pin each strip of boxing-strip batting to the wrong side of each fabric boxing strip with one long edge of each even. Baste all edges of batting to fabric. With wrong sides of fabric together and batting sandwiched between, baste long edges of each boxing strip together.

5. Pin and baste folded edge of each boxing strip to edges of zipper, overlapping ¼ inch. Use zipper foot to stitch zipper to strips (Figure 6).

Figure 6

6. Place end batting on wrong side of lining fabric. Layer right side of end print fabric over batting. Pin and baste all layers together, sandwiching batting between the lining and the fabric (Figure 7).

Figure 7

7. With right sides of fabric together, pin and stitch one short edge of each layered end to each short edge of zippered boxing strip. Clean-finish seams and press toward ends (Figure 8). Topstitch seam allowance to end fabric.

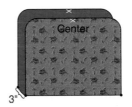

Figure 8

8. Mark center of boxing strip and centers of body at top. With top edges of body even, find the center bottom of body; at edges, mark 1½ inches on each side of center at seam line (Figure 9). Staystitch 2 inches beyond center mark on each side. Clip seam allowance to dots on each side.

Figure 9

9. Unzip zipper slightly. With right sides together and piping sandwiched between, begin at centers and pin boxing strip to body, clipping seam allowance of boxing strip to ease around curves. Stitch boxing strip to body (Figure 10). Trim boxing strip even with seam allowance if needed. Clean-finish seams.

Figure 10

10. Unzip and turn bag right side out. ⏱

Sources: *Soft Touch cotton batting from Fairfield Processing Corp.; sport zipper from Coats & Clark.*

Express Yourself

Designs by Missy Shepler

Quick-to-construct bags are just the right size for trying out new techniques and great for using up bits and pieces of past projects! Insert a gift of money inside, and gift giving has never been simpler.

Estimated Time
3 hours

Bags

Finished sizes
Small Bag: 3¾ x 4¼ inches
Large Bag: 5¾ x 6¼ inches

Materials
- Scrap cotton canvas or denim for bag front
- Scrap coordinating cotton fabric for bag back
- Scrap lightweight cotton fabric for lining
- Scrap cotton batting
- Handle embellishments and tools:
     18-, 20- and 32-gauge craft wire
     assorted beads
     wire cutters
     needle-nose pliers
- Stencil supplies:
     2-inch-wide masking tape
     sharp craft knife
     artist's paintstiks
     parchment paper
     optional: tweezers
     stencil brush or rubber-tipped shaping tool
- Basic sewing supplies and equipment

Project Note: Instructions for both bags are the same. Dimensions for large bag are shown in parentheses throughout.

Cutting
Before cutting, machine-wash and dry fabrics without fabric softener.

From cotton canvas or denim for bag front:
- Cut one 4½ x 4½-inch (6½ x 6½-inch) square.

From coordinating cotton fabric for bag back:
- Cut one 4½ x 4½-inch (6½ x 6½-inch) square.

From lightweight cotton fabric for lining:
- Cut one 4½ x 9-inch (6½ x 13-inch) rectangle.

From batting:
- Cut one 4½ x 4½-inch (6½ x 6½-inch) square.

Quick Tip

Use the patterns provided, print a decorative font from your computer, or clip lettering styles from magazine and newspaper ads. Large lettering works best for stenciling. Avoid ornate, hard-to-cut styles. Fonts with a handwritten look work well, since the rougher style helps hide cutting imperfections.

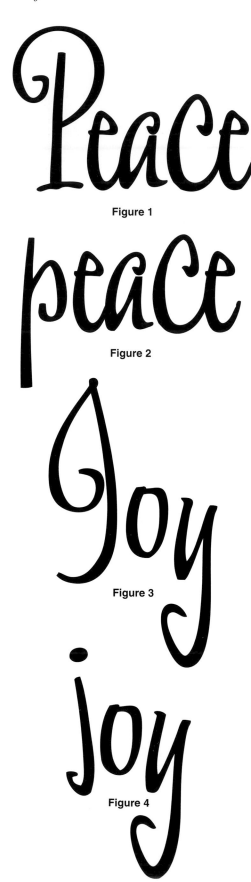

Figure 1

Figure 2

Figure 3

Figure 4

Stencil

1. Place printed text (Figures 1–4) right side up on cutting mat. Lightly place a piece of 2-inch-wide masking tape over lettering and cut out lettering with sharp craft knife. ***Note:*** *To prevent masking tape from adhering too tightly to printed text, adhere a layer of clear packing tape before placing masking tape over lettering.*

2. Be sure to save spaces inside o's, a's, e's, etc. Gently peel masking tape away from cut letters, taking care not to stretch tape. Both the letter forms and the cut stencil can be used as paint-resists.

3. Place masking-tape stencil on bag front. Tweezers may be helpful for positioning smaller stencil pieces. Make sure tape is securely adhered to fabric. ***Note:*** *If desired, torn masking tape makes a simple and easy way to create an interesting border.*

4. Paint stencil (see Paintstiks on page 67). Allow painted fabric to dry a minimum of 24 hours, then remove masking-tape stencil. ***Note:*** *Drying time is dependent on paint thickness. Some paintings may require longer drying times. Three to five days drying time are recommended to allow painted fabrics to cure.*

5. Heat-set dried painting by sandwiching fabric, painted side down, between two pieces of parchment paper. Press entire area 10–15 seconds with a dry iron set at hottest temperature the fabric can withstand. ***Note:*** *Protect ironing surface with parchment paper to prevent staining should any paint seep out of the fabric.*

Assembly

Use ¼-inch wide seam allowances.

1. If desired, add decorative stitching or embellishments to front of bag after stenciling.

2. Layer bag back, right side up, on batting and quilt as desired.

3. With right sides together, stitch bag front to bag back around side and bottom edges. Clip bottom corners. Turn and press.

4. Fold lining right sides together to form a square. Press. With folded edge at bottom, stitch left side seam. Stitch right side seam, leaving an opening for turning.

5. With outer bag right side out, tuck outer bag inside lining so right side of outer bag and right side of lining are together. With top raw edges even and side seams matching, pin together, off-setting side seams slightly to reduce bulk. Stitch bag and lining together around top. Pull outer bag through lining opening.

Handle & Embellishment

1. Use wire cutters to cut a length of 18- or 20-gauge wire 16 (20) inches long. Coil ends and add extra loops as desired by wrapping wire tightly around a pencil or other similar object.

Wrap wire around a jar or can to form the handle arc.

2. Using a needle and thread, stitch ends of handle to sides of bag. ***Note:*** *Insert needle through opening in lining so stitching will not show inside bag.*

3. String beads on thread or 32-gauge wire and attach as desired.

4. Press lining. Hand-stitch opening closed. Turn lining inside bag, folding it over the top seam allowance to create a contrast border. ⏱

Sources: Natural and bleached cotton duck from Dharma Trading Co.; cotton batting from The Warm Company; Shiva artist's paintstiks from Blick Art Supplies; wire from Darice; beads from Blue Moon Beads.

Paintstiks

Paintstiks are oil paint in a solid stick form. The paint's buttery consistency makes blending a breeze, and the stick form eliminates the unpleasant odor and mess usually associated with oil painting.

Paintstiks are self-sealing and will form a thin outer layer of dry paint when exposed to air. Before painting, peel away film with a craft knife or pinch away film with a paper towel.

Colors may be applied directly to the fabric surface or blended on a palette and then applied with a stencil brush or shaper. One easy technique is to layer colors, starting with the lightest color and working toward the darkest tones.

Use a stencil brush or rubber-tipped shaper to gently scrub the first paint color into the fabric. Layer additional colors, blending the paint together between layers.

Waxed paper makes a handy, easy-to-clean palette.

A Snowy Welcome

Design by Denise Clason

Warm your hearts and those of your visitors with this happy snowman appliquéd to a traditional patchwork block. Use it to embellish the front of a metal bucket to hang on your front door, or use indoors for a place to tuck holiday greetings.

Estimated Time
6 hours

Snowman Block

Finished size
12 x 12 inches, excluding the handle

Materials
- Quilter's cotton fabric in tone-on-tone prints:
    - 4 fat quarters, each a different beige
    - 4 fat quarters, each a different green
    - 4 fat quarters, each a different gold
    - 4 fat quarters, each a different red
    - scrap orange print for nose
    - scrap white for face
- 14 x 14-inch square lightweight cotton batting
- 9 x 12-inch sheet paper-backed fusible web
- Optional: ¼-inch-wide paper-backed fusible web tape
- 2 (¼-inch) black shank buttons for eyes
- Gold metallic embroidery floss
- Red yarn for pompom
- 1½ x 4-inch piece cardboard for pompom
- 12-inch square metal wall bucket with hanger
- ⅜ yard bead fringe
- 1 (2-ounce) bottle barn red acrylic paint
- 1 (1-inch-wide) flat paintbrush
- 2-ounce bottle jewel glue
- Wedge-shaped makeup sponge
- Antique gold gilder's paste
- ¼-inch presser foot (recommended)
- Basic sewing tools and equipment

Project Note: *If preferred, use one print instead of four different ones for the green, gold and red prints for the block pieces. Cut the 14-inch backing square from the green or the gold fat quarter and enough binding strips from the remainder of the red fat quarter to make one 55-inch-long strip.*

Cutting
From each of the four beige fat quarters:
- Cut one 4½ x 4½-inch square.

From each of the four green fat quarters:
- Cut one 2½ x 8½-inch rectangle.
- Cut one 2⅞ x 2⅞-inch square.

From each of the four gold fat quarters:
• Cut one 2⅞ x 2⅞-inch square.
• Cut one 2½ x 2½-inch square.

From each of the four red fat quarters:
• Cut two 2½ x 2½-inch squares.

From one of the fat quarters:
• Cut one 14 x 14-inch square for the backing.

From one of the red fat quarters:
• Cut 2¼-inch strips the width of the fabric to equal 55 inches when joined for binding.

Block Assembly

Use ¼-inch-wide seam allowances.

1. Arrange the beige 4½ x 4½-inch squares in two rows of two squares each. Sew the squares together in rows and press the seams in opposite directions. Sew the rows together to complete the four-patch center square (Figure 1). Press the center seam in one direction.

Figure 1

2. On the wrong side of each of the four 2½ x 2½-inch gold squares, draw a diagonal line from corner to corner. With right sides facing, position a gold square at each corner of the Four-Patch block as shown and stitch on the drawn line. Cut away the excess triangle ¼ inch beyond the stitching (Figure 2). Press the triangles toward the seam allowances

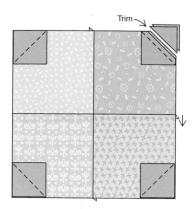

Figure 2

3. Draw a diagonal line on each of the four red 2½ x 2½-inch squares as for the gold squares. Position and sew a red square to the short ends of each of the four green rectangles. Trim and press the seams toward the seam allowances (Figure 3).

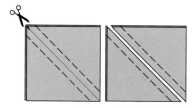

Figure 3

4. Place the 2⅞ x 2⅞-inch green and gold squares together with right sides facing. On the gold square, draw a diagonal line. Using the ¼-inch presser foot, if available, stitch ¼ inch from the line on each side. Cut apart on the drawn line to yield two half-square triangle units (Figure 4).

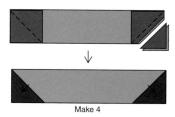

Figure 4

5. Arrange the pieces for the block and sew together in rows as shown in Figure 5. Press the seams in the top and bottom rows toward the corner square. Press the seams in the center row toward the Four-Patch block in the center. Sew the rows together to complete the block and press the seams toward the block center.

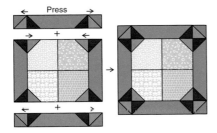

Figure 5

Snowman Appliqué & Quilting

1. Enlarge the appliqué pieces (page 72) and trace onto the paper side of the 9 x 12-inch sheet of fusible web. Leave ½ inch of space between pieces. Cut out each shape, leaving a ¼-inch-wide margin. ***Note:*** *You should have one hat, two hearts, one nose and one face. The lines on the hat are for embroidered details, and the mouth will be machine-stitched.*

2. Apply each piece to the wrong side of the appropriate-color fabric as noted on the templates, following the manufacturer's directions. Cut out each piece on the drawn line.

3. On the fabric side of the snowman face, lightly draw the placement lines for the eyes, nose and mouth. Trace the embroidery lines on the right side of the hat.

4. Remove the backing paper on each piece. Arrange the appliqués on the Four-Patch block, allowing room above the hat for the pompom. Cover with a press cloth and fuse in place following the manufacturer's directions.

5. Adjust the sewing machine for a narrow satin stitch and stitch over the outer edges of each appliqué. Use an even narrower satin stitch for the mouth line.

6. With the embroidery needle and 2 strands of gold metallic floss, backstitch along the detail lines on the hat.

Block Finishing

1. Apply a light coat of temporary spray adhesive to the wrong side of the 14 x 14-inch backing square. Smooth the batting in place on top. Apply a light coat of adhesive to the batting. Center the snowman square on top and smooth into place, keeping the seams and edges straight and perpendicular to each other.

2. Free-motion-quilt the block using transparent thread. Stitch around the edge of the snowman, hat and facial features. Trim excess batting and backing matching the edges of the block.

3. Fold the binding strip in half lengthwise with wrong sides facing and press. Open and turn under the end at a 45-degree angle.

4. Beginning in the center of one side of the block, pin and sew the binding to the right side with raw edges even. Miter the corners as you reach them. Trim the excess binding, leaving enough to tuck into the opening at the beginning of the binding. Complete the stitching (Figure 6). Press the binding toward the seams.

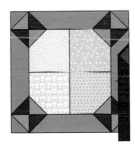

Figure 6

5. Flip the block over and wrap the binding to the underside. Hand-sew or use ¼-inch-wide fusible web tape to fuse the binding to the back of the block.

6. Cut a 12½-inch-long piece of bead fringe. Tuck the header of the bead fringe under the lower edge of the block. Turn under the ends at each side of the block for a neat finish, and stitch in the ditch of the binding seam and again through the center of the binding using transparent thread. Sew the buttons in place for the eyes.

7. To make the pompom, cut a 5-inch-long piece of red yarn and lay it at the 4-inch edge of the 1½ x 4-inch cardboard form. Wrap red yarn around 30–40 times. Tie the ends of the 5-inch piece in a tight knot. Cut the yarn loops along the opposite edge of the cardboard. Trim all yarn ends as needed to shape the pompom to the size desired (Figure 7). Glue the pompom at the top of the hat.

Figure 7

Painting the Bucket

1. Use the 1-inch-wide flat paintbrush to apply two coats of barn red paint to both sides of the wall bucket and the hanger, letting dry after each coat.

2. Use a wedge-shaped makeup sponge to brush gold gilder's paste over the edges of the bucket and the handle.

3. Glue the quilted block to the tin and allow to dry.

4. Tuck holiday greenery into the bucket if desired. ⏱

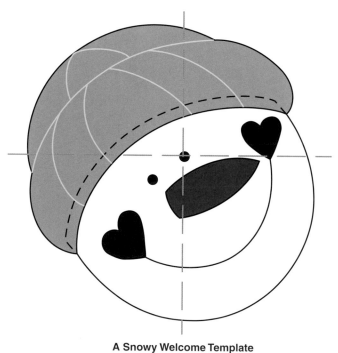

A Snowy Welcome Template
Enlarge 200%

Tumbling Blocks
Blanket

Design by Leslie Hartsock

Not only warm and fuzzy, but so fast and easy that, while you're at it, you may want to make several of these blankets to ensure that you always have a baby gift on hand.

Estimated Time
4 hours

Blanket

Finished size
36 x 36 inches

Materials
• 36 x 36-inch square yellow fleece
• Scraps fabric for appliqué:
    yellow
    light blue
    dark blue
    light pink
    dark pink
    purple
    orange
    green
• 2 skeins 6-strand mint green embroidery floss
• Rayon machine-embroidery thread
• ¼ yard paper-backed fusible web
• ⅓ yard tear-away fabric stabilizer
• Basic sewing supplies and equipment

Instructions
1. Use a salad plate to round off the corners of the fleece square.

2. Trace appliqué shapes onto paper side of fusible web as directed on templates; cut out, leaving roughly ½-inch margin around shapes.

3. Fuse to wrong side of selected fabrics according to manufacturer's directions; cut out on traced lines.

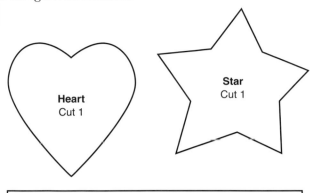

Heart
Cut 1

Star
Cut 1

Outside Block
Cut 8
(reverse 4)

Inside Block
Cut 8

4. Using photo as a guide, position appliqué pieces; fuse in place.

Note: *Appliqués on model project were stitched using all-purpose thread in bobbin and rayon machine-embroidery thread in top.*

5. Pin tear-away fabric stabilizer behind appliqué area. Satin-stitch around each appliqué, beginning with background pieces and working forward. Carefully tear away stabilizer.

6. Using 6 strands of mint green embroidery floss, work buttonhole stitch around edges of fleece. ***Note:*** *Edges do not need to be turned under.* ○

Cut 1

Cut 1

Cut 1

Cut 1

Cut 1

Cut 1

Tumbling Blocks Blanket Templates

No-Sweat Work-Out Mat

Designs by Cheryl Stranges

Cut fabric strips, serge and weave for a quick finish on this no-sweat work-out mat. Give as a gift to young moms who will love the soft mat to exercise with small children or to spend an energetic afternoon exercising as children nap.

Estimated Time
5 hours

Mat

Finished sizes
Woven throw assembly:
37 x 25 inches
Pad Cover: 40 x 26 inches

Materials
- 45-inch-wide woven fabric:
    - 1½ yards bright-print cotton
    - 1 yard coordinating soft-print cotton
    - 2½ yards cotton solid
- Scrap bright contrast-color cotton
- 60-inch-wide knit fabric:
    - 1½ yards soft-knit fleece
    - 1 yard lamb-look soft-knit fleece
- 37 x 25 inches 1-inch-thick foam
- Cotton ink-jet fabric sheets
- Computer photograph or print
- Lightweight cut- or tear-away stabilizer
- 2 inches 1-inch-wide hook-and-loop tape
- 3D or 4D embroidery software
- Alphabet embroidery design
- 60 inches ¼-inch-wide coordinating ribbon*
- Sewing feet:
    - nonstick glide (Teflon) foot to sew photos
    - edgestitching foot
- Coordinating threads for serger**
- 1 spool black metallic thread for embroidery letters
- 60-weight black bobbin thread
- Optional: Invisible thread
- 240 x 150cm embroidery hoop
- Basic sewing supplies and equipment

*Yardage given borders a 4¾ x 6¾-inch photo or print appliqué on model project. Adjust accordingly for larger or smaller appliqués.
**Rayon threads were used for decorative sheen on model project.

Project Note: *Prewash fabrics before you start. Tip: Finish all of your raw edges on your fabric pieces using your serger before you wash them.*

Cutting

From bright-print cotton:
• Cut seven 4 x 40-inch strips.

From soft-knit fleece:
• Cut seven 5 x 45-inch strips.

From lamb-look soft-knit fleece:
• Cut 10 (4 x 29-inch) strips.

From coordinating soft-print cotton:
• Cut 10 (5 x 29-inch) strips.

From cotton solid:
• Cut two 27 x 41-inch rectangles for foam pad cover front and back.

From coordinating ribbon:
• Cut four 15-inch lengths.

Embroidery

Make one for throw and one for pad cover.

1. Following manufacturer's instructions, prepare embroidery software font and words that you wish to print. ***Note:*** *To save time, you can organize multiple words on your computer screen, and transfer the design to your sewing machine. See your sewing machine manual.*

2. Using black metallic thread and 60-weight bobbin thread, stitch out embroidery fonts using bright contrast-color cotton and light- to mediumweight stabilizer in hoop. When complete, cut out words leaving at least ¾ inch around edges. Using rolled hem on serger, serge around two long sides of word first and then two short sides. Leave a chain on each corner; apply seam sealant and let dry.

Photo Ink-Jet

Make one for throw and one for pad cover.

1. Following manufacturer's instructions, print desired photo or print onto ink-jet fabric.

2. Edge finish as in step 2 for embroidery.

Woven Throw Assembly

1. Spray-baste one 4 x 40-inch bright-print cotton strip to one 5 x 45-inch soft-knit fleece strip, wrong sides together. ***Note:*** *Center the cotton so the knit shows ½ inch on each side of the cotton (Figure 1). This will allow you to serge the fabrics together using a 3- or 4-thread overlock finish and trim the excess knit away leaving the cotton at a 4-inch width.*

Figure 1

2. Spray-baste lamb-look fleece and soft-print cotton strips together in same manner as in step 1.

3. Serge strips together along long edges, working with cotton strips on the top.

4. Referring to photo, weave strips together, keeping strips close to each other. Pin strips all around outer edges and trim pieces extending 1 inch beyond edge.

5. Tuck right sides of end pieces under and pin to back strip running underneath. Tuck wrong side of pieces facing upward to strips running on top. Using your edgestitching foot, stitch around outside edges with edge of strips along the flange on the foot and needle in center position.

6. Set your sewing machine to a short length zig-zag. Stitch each intersection of the strips to secure.

7. Position ink-jet photo appliqué and embroidered appliqué as desired on top of throw. Lightly spray-baste in place. Tuck rolled-edge chains under appliqués. Straight-stitch around edges of appliqués using invisible thread.

8. Center a length of ribbon over each side of photo appliqué and sew using invisible thread and decorative stitching, straight stitch or zigzag stitch. Tie ends of ribbons into bows at corners of photo appliqué.

Pad Cover Assembly

1. Position ink-jet photo appliqué and embroidered appliqué as desired on pad cover front and spray-baste in place. Straight-stitch around edges using invisible thread.

2. Using a rolled edge, sew pad cover front and back with wrong sides together along two long and one short edge, leaving one end open for inserting foam pad. On open edge, use a rolled edge around single-layer edge. Sew hook-and-loop-tape fastener centered on opening edge. Place foam pad inside cover. ○

Sources: *Husqvarna Viking embroidery software and Embroidery #146 Modern Alphabet by Ann-Sofie Dreij were used for model project.*

On the Roll
Checkers Game

Design by June McCrary Jacobs

Sew this adorable fabric checker set before your family leaves town. Remember to pack your bags, round up the kids or grandkids, and roll up the fabric checkers set to keep children of all ages occupied during your trip.

Checkers Game

Finished sizes
Checkerboard: 14¾ x 14¾ inches
Checker: 1¼ inches in diameter

Materials
- 60-inch-wide acrylic felt:
    - ¾ yard black
    - ¼ yard light pink
    - ¼ yard hot pink
    - ¼ yard white
- 1½ yards ⅝-inch-wide black grosgrain ribbon
- 1 yard black 6-strand embroidery floss
- 1¼-inch decorative buttons:
    - 2 pink
    - 2 blue
- 4 size 4 black metal snap fasteners
- Basic sewing supplies and equipment

Cutting
From black felt:
- Cut four 2 x 16-inch strips for checkerboard.
- Cut one 15½ x 15½-inch square for backing.
- Cut four 7 x 9-inch rectangles for pockets and pocket linings.

From light pink felt:
- Cut four 2 x 16-inch strips for checkerboard.
- Cut two 2 x 15½-inch strips for long borders.
- Cut two 2 x 12½-inch strips for short borders.

From hot pink felt:
• Cut 12 (3½ x 3½-inch) squares for checkers.

From white felt:
• Cut 12 (3½ x 3½-inch) squares for checkers.

From black grosgrain ribbon:
• Cut two 24-inch lengths for ties.

Checkerboard Assembly

Use ¼-inch-wide seam allowances unless otherwise stated. Use a short machine stitch and black thread unless otherwise stated.

1. Sew one light pink and one black 2 x 16-inch strip together lengthwise. Make four units.

2. Sew black/light pink units together, alternating colors. Press, using acrylic setting on iron.

3. Using rotary cutter, cut across seams to make eight 2 x 12½-inch strips.

4. Sew strips together so pink and black checks alternate. Square should measure 12½ x 12½ inches. Press.

5. Sew short border strips across two opposite sides of checkerboard, matching raw edges. Press.

6. Sew long border strips across remaining sides of checkerboard in same manner (Figure 1). Press.

Figure 1

7. Using a round object as a template (jar, lid, glass, etc.), trim two top corners of each pocket and pocket lining rectangle using the photograph as a reference. Position pocket and pocket lining

with wrong sides together. Using a medium stitch length, sew pocket pieces together across rounded top edges and across bottom edges, leaving seam allowances exposed for trim. Repeat for second set.

8. Fold bottom of each pocket up 3¼ inches; pin in place. Position pockets side by side on backing, 1 inch from bottom edge and ¾ inch from each side. Sew pockets to backing down each side and across bottoms.

9. Sew snaps to pockets and pocket flaps for closures. Sew decorative buttons on outside of pocket flaps over snaps using black embroidery floss.

10. Sew 24-inch lengths of grosgrain ribbon to back of backing piece as shown in Figure 2. Temporarily pin ends of ribbons up so they do not get caught in side seams.

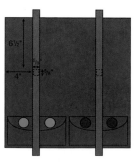

6½"

4"

Figure 2

11. Pin checkerboard and backing right sides together. Sew around edges using a ⅜-inch-wide seam allowance and leaving an opening on one side for turning.

12. Trim corners and turn right side out. Press. Slipstitch opening closed. Topstitch ¼ inch from outer edges. Unpin ties.

Checkers Assembly

1. Using a 2¾-inch diameter object as a template (jar, glass, lid, etc.), trace a circle on the center of each hot pink and white square of felt. Cut out.

2. Turn edges under ¼ inch. Using ⅜-inch-long stitches and a double strand of matching thread, hand-stitch completely around edge of circle. *Note: Begin stitching with knotted end on the turned-under side of the circle. At knot, take one more stitch beyond it.*

3. Pull thread to gather edges of yo-yo, keeping bottom flat. Knot end of thread securely and cut thread.

4. Store checkers in pockets on back of checkerboard. Roll up checkerboard and tie ribbons to secure. ○

Source: Buttons from Dill Buttons of America Inc.

Leaf Peeper's *Tote*

Design by Pam Lindquist for Coats & Clark

Batik prints in mottled autumn colors are the perfect choice for the leaves falling across the front of this roomy tote. The lined bag features faux leather accents and a roomy interior to accommodate your camera and other essentials. This is a gift you may want to keep for yourself.

Estimated Time
6 hours

Tote

Finished size
15 x 17½ inches, excluding handles

Materials
- 25 (5 x 6-inch) rectangles assorted cotton batik prints in fall colors for leaf blocks
- 44/45-inch-wide fabrics:
    - ⅝ yard brown faux leather or suede for tote back and trim
    - ⅝ yard cotton print or solid for tote lining
- ½ yard 22-inch-wide lightweight fusible interfacing
- 19 x 19-inch square lightweight quilt batting
- 19 x 19-inch square cotton muslin for backing
- ½ yard ³⁄₁₆-inch cotton cable cord for piping
- 6 x 18-inch piece firm fusible nonwoven stabilizer
- 4 (1-inch) buttons
- Optional: walking foot for quilting
- Basic sewing supplies and equipment

Cutting
From each of the 5 x 6-inch batik rectangles for leaf blocks:

Note: *Refer to Figure 1.*

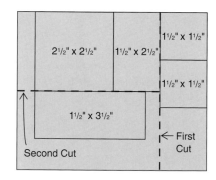

Figure 1

- Cut one 1½ x 5-inch strip; cut two 1½ x 1½-inch squares from the strip.
- Cut one 2½ x 2½-inch square.
- Cut one 1½ x 2½-inch rectangle.
- Cut one 1½ x 3½-inch rectangle.

From brown faux leather or suede:
• Cut two 3 x 18-inch strips for handles.
• Cut one 2 x 15½-inch strip for piping.
• Cut one 7½ x 15½-inch rectangle for upper front band.
• Cut one 15½ x 22½-inch rectangle for tote back.

From cotton print or solid fabric:
• Cut two 14½ x 15½-inch rectangles for tote lining.

From lightweight fusible interfacing:
• Cut two 7 x 15½-inch strips.

From fusible nonwoven stabilizer:
• Cut two 3 x 18-inch rectangles for handles.

Piecing & Quilting

Use ¼-inch-wide seam allowances unless otherwise directed.

1. With a pencil, draw a diagonal line from corner to corner on the wrong side of each 1½ x 1½-inch batik square. Fold 1½ x 1½-inch batik squares in half diagonally temporarily.

2. Referring to Figures 2 and 3 arrange batik pieces to form five rows of five leaf blocks. **Note:** *Examine the photos as well as Figures 2 and 3 to understand how the colors break into the blocks on each side and into the row immediately below them.*

The orientation of the leaves is different in the even and odd rows, and each leaf is cut from a different fabric. Use the extra 1½-inch squares around the outer edges of the layout, positioning the colors to complement the overall design.

Notice how leaf points break into adjacent blocks where circled

Figure 2

Figure 3

3. Unfold 1½-inch squares. Assemble pieces block by block, one row at a time, adding the 1½-inch squares to opposite corners of each 2½-inch square with right sides facing and stitching on the pencil line (Figure 4). Trim the points, leaving a ¼-inch-wide seam allowance. Press the seams toward the remaining triangles.

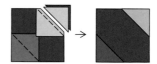

Figure 4

4. Add the side rectangles and press the seams toward the rectangles (Figure 5).

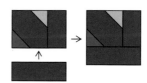

Figure 5

5. Sew the blocks together in horizontal rows and press the seams in opposite directions from row to row so the seams will butt easily at each seam intersection.

6. Sew the rows together, taking care to match the seam intersections. Press the seams toward the bottom of the pieced panel.

7. Place the batting square on top of the muslin square and add the pieced leaf panel on top, right side up. Smooth into place and hand- or pin-baste the layers together for quilting.

8. Hand- or machine-quilt as desired; use a walking foot, if available, for machine quilting. Machine-baste a scant ¼ inch from the outer edges, and then trim the batting and backing fabric even with the outer edges of the pieced panel.

Tote Assembly

1. Wrap the 2 x 15½-inch strip of leather or faux suede around the cotton cable cord, and use a zipper foot to stitch close to the cord (Figure 6). Trim the seam allowance to ¼ inch along the length of the finished piping.

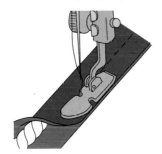

Figure 6

2. Position the piping on the right side at the upper edge of the quilted panel with raw edges even; machine-baste in place close to the cord.

3. Apply the fusible interfacing to the wrong side of the 7½ x 15½-inch rectangle for upper front band and to the upper edge of the 15½ x 22½-inch rectangle for the tote back. Use a press cloth to protect the fabric and test the iron temperature on scraps first.

Note: Refer to Figure 7 for steps 4–6.

4. With right sides facing, sew the interfaced upper front band to the piped edge of the quilted leaf panel. Finger-press the seam toward the quilted panel. Sew a lining rectangle to the remaining edge of the upper front band. Finger-press the seam toward the lining.

5. Sew the remaining lining rectangle to the interfaced upper edge of the tote back.

6. With right sides together, pin and sew the two tote panels together, leaving an 8-inch opening at the bottom edge of the lining.

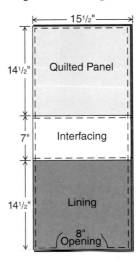

Figure 7

7. Turn the tote right side out through the opening in the lining. Turn under edges of opening and machine-stitch closed.

8. Turn the lining into the tote, leaving a 3-inch-wide band of faux leather or suede above the upper edge of the patchwork. Topstitch ¼ inch from the upper edge of the tote to secure the layers.

9. Apply the fusible stabilizer to the wrong side of each 3 x 18-inch faux leather or suede handle strip. Use a press cloth to avoid damaging the fabric.

10. With wrong sides together, fold the two lengthwise raw edges in toward the center of the strip. Pin in place at each end only. Trim the ends to round the corners (Figure 8). Satin-stitch over the curved raw edges for a neat finish. Remove the pins.

Figure 8

11. Fold each strip in half lengthwise with the raw edges inside. Beginning and ending 3 inches from the ends, stitch the folded edges together to complete each handle (Figure 9).

Figure 9

12. Position the handle ends on the tote front, centering them in the upper band over the first and last seam line in the patchwork row. Stitch in place through all layers in an S-shape as shown in Figure 10. Sew the second handle to the bag back, positioning the ends to match the positioning on the front of the bag. Sew a button over stitching on end of each handle. ⏱

Figure 10

Calm Cat Neck Wrap

Design by Angie Wilhite

Your friends will purr when you give them this rice-filled neck wrap. Simply heat in the microwave, wrap around your neck and feel the worries of the day melt away.

Estimated Time
2 hours

Neck Wrap

Finished size

17 x 8 inches, excluding handles

Materials

- 44-inch-wide woven fabric:
    - ½ yard animal-print for outer bag
    - ½ yard for rice bag
- Scraps woven fabric for appliqués:
    - tan
    - black
    - white
    - red
- Paper-backed fusible web
- Lightweight fusible interfacing
- Tear-away fabric stabilizer
- 20 inches 1-inch-wide black cotton webbing for handles
- Rayon embroidery thread to match fabric
- Black fine-tip permanent marker
- 7 cups long-grain rice
- 5 inches of 1-inch-wide hook-and-loop tape
- Optional: 1 tablespoon orange peel
- Basic sewing supplies and equipment

Cutting

From animal-print fabric:

- Cut one 17 x 18-inch rectangle.

From fabric for rice bag:

- Cut one 14 x 18-inch rectangle.

From scraps woven fabric for appliqués:

- Apply fusible web to wrong sides of fabrics. Use templates provided to cut one head, one body, one tail, two eyes, two pupils and one heart.

Assembly

Use ½-inch-wide seam allowances unless otherwise stated.

1. On both 17-inch edges of animal-print rectangle, fold under and stitch a double-fold ¼-inch hem.

2. With animal-print square face down, fold up one hemmed edge 4 inches and the other hemmed edge 5 inches with wrong sides together; pin in place. Turn over to front of bag. Position appliqué pieces on center front and fuse in place. Remove pins from bag and unfold edges.

3. Pin or baste stabilizer to wrong side of bag behind appliqué pieces. Using rayon embroidery thread for needle thread and matching all-purpose thread in bobbin, satin-stitch around appliqué shapes. Trim threads and remove stabilizer. Using black fine-tip permanent marker, draw whiskers and mouth on cat.

4. With right sides together, refold hemmed edges as before and pin together. Cut webbing in half to make two 10-inch lengths for handles. Slip handles inside bag. Pin ends of each length to one end of bag even with raw edges, positioning 1 inch from folded edges. Sew ends of bag together, catching

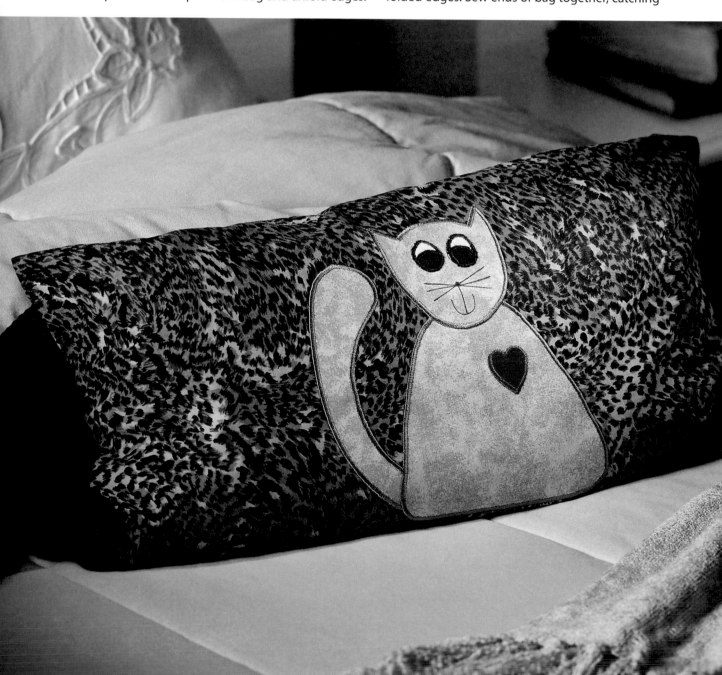

ends of handles in stitching. Clip corners and turn bag right side out. Press. Position hook-and-loop tape along each side of back opening. Sew each strip into place.

5. For rice bag, fold fabric rectangle in half and sew edges together, leaving a 3-inch opening for turning. Clip corners and turn right side out. Fill bag with rice and, if desired, orange peel. Hand-stitch opening closed.

6. To use, place rice bag inside outer bag. Heat in microwave 2 minutes. Use handles to remove from microwave. Place around neck. ○

Sources: *Dual-Duty Plus rayon embroidery thread from Coats & Clark; Wonder-Under fusible web, Sof-Shape fusible interfacing and Stitch-n-Tear fabric stabilizer from Pellon.*

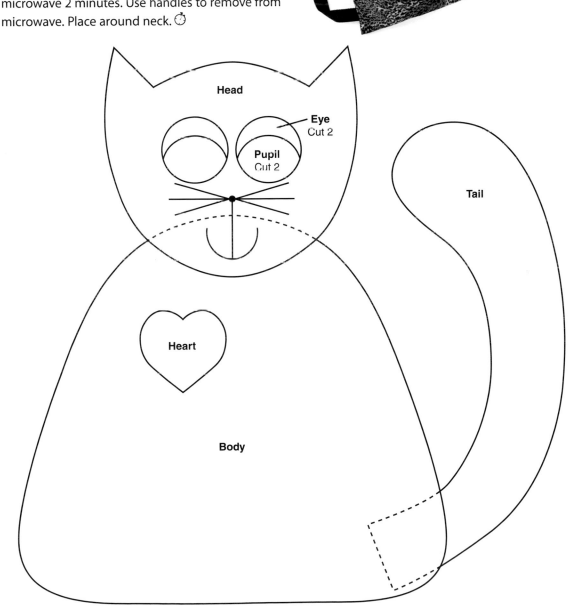

Calm Cat Neck Wrap Templates

I Love Golf & Bowling

Designs by Angie Wilhite

Sew this simple golf or bowling hand towel for the man in your life or as a stylish gift for yourself. He'll love it and love you for your thoughtfulness.

Estimated Time
2 hours

Hand Towels

Finished size
16 x 24-inches

Materials
- 16 x 24-inch hand towel
- Scrap fabrics for appliqués:
    - yellow
    - red
    - neon green
    - white
    - neon orange
    - turquoise
- 4 x 14-inch square paper-backed fusible web
- 4 x 14-inch square tear-away fabric stabilizer
- Rayon embroidery thread
- Basic sewing supplies and equipment

Instructions
1. Prewash towel and fabrics without softener.

2. Following manufacturer's instructions, apply fusible web to backs of appliqué fabrics. Use templates provided to trace each letter/shape onto the paper side of the fusible web. Cut out shapes. Remove paper backing.

3. Position appliqué shapes on lower half of towel. Fuse in place.

4. Pin or baste fabric stabilizer to back of towel behind appliqués. Thread machine with rayon embroidery thread in top and matching all-purpose thread in bobbin.

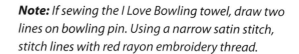

Note: *If sewing the I Love Bowling towel, draw two lines on bowling pin. Using a narrow satin stitch, stitch lines with red rayon embroidery thread.*

5. Using photo as a guide, satin-stitch edges of appliqués, sewing shapes that are behind adjoining shapes first. ⏱

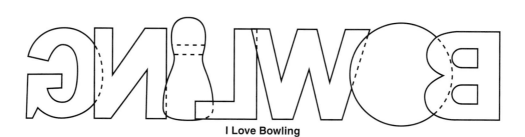

I Love Bowling

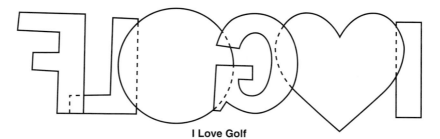

I Love Golf

Towel Templates
Enlarge 200%

Kit & Caboodle
Kitchen Towels

Designs by Carol Zentgraf

The traditional technique of making fabric yo-yos is quick and easy with fun-to-use yo-yo makers in a variety of shapes. They're perfect for embellishing this set of whimsical kitchen towels.

Estimated Time
2½ hours

Kitchen Towels

Finished size
20½ x 29 inches

Materials for one towel
- 1 yard 44/45-inch-wide woven cotton fabric for towel
- Large scraps assorted cotton print fabrics for appliqués and yo-yos
- ⅔ yard fabric rickrack
- Small scraps assorted trims for embellishment
- Yo-yo makers in assorted shapes and sizes
- Paper-backed fusible web
- Permanent fabric adhesive
- Basic sewing supplies and equipment

Cutting
From woven cotton fabric for towel:
- Cut one 21½ x 30-inch rectangle.

From large scrap cotton print fabric for appliqué:
- Apply fusible web to wrong side of fabric. Trace desired vase template (page 96) onto paper side of fusible web and cut out on traced line.

Assembly

1. Press and stitch a double ¼-inch hem in side edges of towel. Repeat for top and bottom edges.

2. Remove paper backing from vase appliqué and position in center lower half of towel. Fuse in place. Satin-stitch around edges of vase.

3. Follow yo-yo-maker instructions to make several yo-yos in desired sizes and shapes from assorted cotton print fabrics. Adhere centers of yo-yos to towel above vase.

4. Using an air- or water-soluble marker, draw a stem from each yo-yo to the vase. Stitch stems with a wide zigzag stitch, being careful not to catch the yo-yo in the stitching.

5. Sew fabric rickrack across bottom front edge of towel, wrapping ends to back.

6. Use permanent fabric adhesive to embellish top of vase with trim. ○

Sources: *Cotton print fabric and fabric rickrack from Michael Miller Fabrics; trims from Expo International; yo-yo makers from Clover Needlecraft; Steam-A-Seam2 fusible web from The Warm Company; Fabri-Tac permanent adhesive from Beacon Adhesives Inc.*

Kit & Caboodle Kitchen Towels Templates
Enlarge 200%

Wine Caddy

Design by Janis Bullis

This wine caddy is so quick and easy to make you'll want to make one for everyone on your gift list. A large plastic snap-in-place drapery grommet serves as the handle, and various-size wine bottles slip into place through the side opening.

Estimated Time
1 hour

Caddy

Finished size
7 x 16 inches

Materials
- 7 x 32 inches nonwoven fabric
- 2 sets (2¾-inch inside diameter) plastic drapery grommets
- 4-pound handheld sledge hammer and 2 (6-inch) square wooden boards (to set grommets)
- Basic sewing supplies and equipment

Instructions
1. Place a grommet at each end of fabric, centered side to side and 1 inch from end. (Figure 1). Trace inside each grommet; cut out center fabric on traced line.

Figure 1

2. Working on the floor or a very sturdy surface, place large grommet half, wrong side up, centered on one wooden board. With fabric facing right

side up, gently stretch opening cut in step 1 over grommet and around lip into outside ridge. Place remaining small grommet half, wrong side down, centered over the assembly.

3. Gently rest the second board over the assembly. Using the sledge hammer, swing one hard blow to the center of the board to snap the grommet halves into place, pinching the fabric between the halves. Repeat for the second grommet set.

4. With wrong sides of the fabric and grommets facing, fold fabric in half crosswise (Figure 2). With all cut edges even, pin long sides together. Topstitch sides, stopping 6 inches from fold at bottom. Secure threads.

Figure 2

5. To use, insert wine bottle through opening at side edge. ☼

Source: *Drapery grommets from Drapery Sewing Supplies.*

Be Cozy
Felted Tea Cozy

Design by Zoe Graul

Felt two old wool sweaters from your closet or from a resale shop to make a dense but soft and textural fabric—then have fun sewing this quick and functional cozy. Be sure to make several; this is a simple-to-sew gift, perfect for the holiday season.

Estimated Time
1 hour

Tea Cozy

Finished size
Approximately 19 inches in circumference x 7 inches tall

Materials
- 100 percent wool sweaters*
   1 sweater for cozy (MC)
   1 sweater for flower (CC)
- 45 inches ⅜-inch-wide grosgrain ribbon
- 1–1½-inch decorative button
- 2 old pillowcases or mesh laundry bags
- 2 rubber bands
- Basic sewing supplies and equipment

Sweaters must be 100 percent wool or they will not felt properly.

Preparation
1. Place each sweater in a separate pillowcase and close pillowcases with rubber bands. Felt each sweater separately (to avoid color bleeding) by laundering with detergent.

Note: Use regular setting and small/medium load. Add a couple of old items to balance the load.

2. Run through at least one complete cycle. Check to see if felting is dense enough. Run through an additional cycle if needed.

3. Place each sweater on a towel. Smooth and flatten sweater; roll up towel with sweater inside, adding pressure to remove as much water as possible. Unroll and let sweaters air-dry.

4. Cut sweaters apart at seams. Select side of fabric you wish to use as the right side and mark with a pin.

Cutting
Model project fits a rounded 4-cup teapot measuring approximately 17½ inches around (excluding handle and spout) and 6½ inches high. Adjust pattern for tea cozy accordingly for teapots with other measurements.

From MC fabric:
• Use template to cut four tea cozy pieces, marking right sides.

From CC fabric:
• Use template to cut one flower.

Assembly

Use ½-inch-wide seam allowances.

Sew pieces with wrong sides together. Seam allowances are on the outside of the cozy.

1. Sew two tea cozy pieces together along one curved edge. Repeat with remaining two pieces.

2. Pin both halves together, matching seams at top. Place cozy over teapot (Figure 1).

Figure 1

3. Mark placement of spout and handles. Stitch seam for spout from top to spout and from bottom edge to spout. Stitch seam for handle from top only, leaving remainder of seam open to bottom edge.

4. Pin ⅜-inch-wide grosgrain ribbon to inside bottom edge of cozy, centering ribbon at seam under spout (Figure 2). Stitch ribbon to cozy along both edges, keeping seam allowances open.

Figure 2

5. Flatten seams at top of cozy. Hand-stitch flower to top. Sew decorative button to center of flower. ⏱

Quick Tips

Make two cozies from the sweaters by reversing the main and contrasting colors.

Embellish the top of the cozy with a pom-pom or with a cluster of buttons or beads instead of the decorative button.

Make the flower from a scrap of felt or polar fleece instead of using a second sweater.

Flower
Cut 1

Tea Cozy
Cut 4

Be Cozy Felted Tea Cozy Templates

Sophisticated Soap

Designs by Linda Turner Griepentrog

Any hostess wants a talked-about event, and these special embroidered soaps are sure to spark conversation. These make treasured gifts too. The small embroidered soaps are unique stocking stuffers and can be made as a set or individually.

Estimated Time
2 hours

Soap

Finished size

Varies, depending on embroidery design selected

Materials

- Machine-embroidery designs
- Optional: tulle or organza to match soaps*
- Clear water-soluble stabilizer
- Decorative soaps
- Optional: paraffin
- Sharp-point embroidery scissors
- Basic sewing supplies and equipment

*If using a freestanding embroidery design, omit tulle or organza.

Project note: *Soap bars with recessed tops work well, but indented branding or logos should be avoided. Often, the underside of a bar is smooth if the top is not.*

Preparation

Turn soap bars upside down in a shallow dish of water to soften upper surface.

Embroidery

1. Hoop the water-soluble stabilizer and tulle or organza.

2. Stitch embroidered motif. Trim jump threads on upper and lower surfaces.

3. Trim fabric and stabilizer very close to design outer edge, but avoid cutting any stitches. **Note:** *If design has interior openings, it is not necessary to trim these. They will disappear into the soap surface when the design is applied.*

Assembly

1. Turn softened soap surface upward and embed trimmed embroidered motif into surface, smoothing it into place to remove wrinkles. **Note:** *Remove any visible stabilizer by spritzing with water to dissolve.*

2. Set soap aside one hour to dry, checking on it periodically to make sure embroidery adheres smoothly to surface, especially at edges. Press motif into the soap surface as it dries and smooth ragged soap edges, as well, for a polished look.

Option: Add a thin layer of melted paraffin to the dry upper soap surface for protection. ⏱

Sources: *Tiny Winter Holidays 2 embroidery design from Perfect Little Stitches; Miniatures embroidery designs from Smart Needle; Solvy water-soluble stabilizer from Sulky of America.*

Lace Motif

If your machine doesn't have embroidery capabilities, try following the same steps with purchased appliqués or create your own appliqués by carefully cutting a motif from lace.

Just for Fun

Washing with embroidered soaps will cause the design to separate from the surface. If placing these sweetly scented accents on the lavatory, leave a tiny "Just for Fun" sign nearby to let guests know they are purely decorative.

Sachet Heart *Appliqué Bags*

Design by Angie Wilhite

Appliqué, sew, and fill these small sachet bags with sweet-smelling potpourri. Create a set, gift-wrap with care and everyone will know that this gift is from the heart.

Estimated Time
2 hours

Sachet Bags

Finished size
3½ x 4¾ inches

Materials for one bag

- 5 x 8-inch piece white linen
- Scraps coordinating solid and floral print woven fabric for appliqué
- ¼ yard ⅝-inch-wide white decorative trim
- ½ yard ⅛-inch-wide satin ribbon
- Embellishments:
    key charm
    heart button
    ribbon rose
- Potpourri
- Scraps of fusible web
- Scraps of tear-away fabric stabilizer
- Rayon embroidery thread
- Permanent fabric adhesive
- Basic sewing supplies and equipment

Instructions

Use ¼-inch-wide seam allowances unless otherwise stated.

1. With raw edges even, sew trim to right side of linen along one 8-inch edge. Press seam toward linen; topstitch.

2. Apply fusible web to wrong sides of fabric scraps. Use template provided to cut solid and printed heart pieces.

3. Fold linen in half, matching 5-inch edges; press. Open and lay right side up. Position heart pieces on front of bag and fuse in place. Pin or baste stabilizer to wrong side of bag behind appliqué. Using rayon thread as the top thread and matching all-purpose thread in the bobbin, satin-stitch around edges of appliqué pieces. Remove stabilizer.

4. With right sides together, sew side and bottom seams of bag. Turn right side out and press. Cut a 6-inch length of ribbon and tie in a bow. Sew and/or glue embellishments to appliqué.

5. Fill bag with potpourri. Tie closed with a 12-inch length of ribbon. ⏱

Sources: *Dual-Duty Plus rayon embroidery thread from Coats & Clark; Wonder-Under fusible web and Stitch-n-Tear fabric stabilizer from Pellon; Gem-Tac permanent adhesive from Beacon Adhesives Inc.*

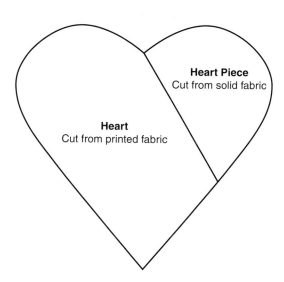

Sachet Heart Appliqué Bags Templates

Cherish the Moment Journal

Design by Holly Daniels

What better way to collect family and friends' memorabilia than to create a customized journal for each guest highlighting the event. Your journal will become a cherished keepsake helping keep your memories alive long after the event is over.

Estimated Time
3 hours

Journal

Finished size
7¾ x 10½ inches

Materials
- ½ yard 44-inch-wide pink floral print woven fabric for cover
- Coordinating woven fabric:
    - 2 (3 x 3-inch) squares green floral print for flower petal background
    - 2 (3 x 3-inch) squares light green polka dot for flower petal background
    - 5 x 5-inch square light pink floral print for small petals
    - 5 x 5-inch square dark pink floral print for large petals
    - 1 fat quarter green polka dot for piping
- 5½ x 2½-inch piece white solid woven fabric
- 90 inches cord for piping
- 4 x 4-inch square lightweight paper-backed fusible web

- Embroidery floss:
    - green
    - light pink
    - medium pink
- 7⅜ x 9⅝-inch composition notebook
- Basic sewing supplies and equipment

Cutting
From pink floral print for cover:
- Cut one 16½ x 11-inch rectangle for outside cover.
- Cut one 5 x 11-inch rectangle for lining.
- Cut two 8 x 11-inch rectangles for inside flaps.

From light pink floral print for small petals:
• Use template provided to trace five small petals on paper side of fusible web; cut out. Fuse onto wrong side of fabric. Cut out.

From dark pink floral print for large petals:
• Use template provided to trace five large petals on paper side of fusible web; cut out. Fuse onto wrong side of fabric. Cut out.

From green polka dot for piping:
• Cut 2-inch-wide strips on the bias to equal 90 inches total when joined for piping.

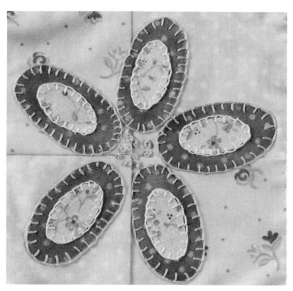

Assembly

Use ¼-inch-wide seam allowances unless otherwise stated.

1. Sew one green floral print and one green polka dot 3 x 3-inch square together. Repeat with remaining 3 x 3-inch squares; sew both pairs together to form flower-petal background.

2. Remove paper backing from flower petals. Fuse large petals into place on background piece, referring to photo for placement. Fuse small petals in centers of large petals.

3. Using 2 strands of embroidery floss, hand-embroider a decorative blanket stitch around edge of each petal using light pink floss around small petals and medium pink floss around large petals; work French knots in flower center using light pink and medium pink floss. Trim background to 5½ x 5½ inches with flower in center.

4. Sew 2-inch-wide bias strips together on the bias. Cover cord with bias strip to make piping. Cut a 26-inch length of piping. Pin to flower background with raw edges even; stitch in place close to piping, leaving 1 inch unattached at beginning and end. Remove stitches from extra piping fabric and expose cord. Cut cord so ends butt together. Smooth fabric back over cord, overlapping the beginning end and turning raw edge under. Complete stitching the piping to the background fabric.

5. Transfer lettering for "Cherish" to 5½ x 2½-inch white fabric rectangle. Embroider with outline or split stitch using 2 strands of green embroidery floss. Work French knot to dot "i". Turn under raw edges ¼ inch; press.

6. Place 16½ x 11-inch rectangle of pink floral print for outside cover right side up. Center flower block and word block on right-hand side of fabric for front of book. Pin or baste in place. Stitch pieces to front using blanket stitch and 2 strands of floss—light pink for flower block and medium pink for word block.

7. To make inside flaps, stitch a double-fold ¼-inch hem on one long edge of each 8 x 11-inch rectangle of pink floral print for inside flaps. ***Option:*** *Use a decorative machine stitch for hem.*

8. Pin piping around outside edge of floral print cover with raw edges even. Sew (use zipper foot if needed) and finish as detailed in step 4. Place flaps on outside cover with right sides together, aligning unhemmed edges of flaps with ends

and sides of cover. Place the 5 x 11-inch lining rectangle in center of cover over hemmed edges of flaps. Sew close to piping, finishing as for piping on flower block as shown in Figure 1.

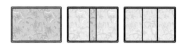

Figure 1

9. Turn cover right side out; press. Insert covers of composition notebook in flaps to use. ⏱

Source: *HeatnBond Lite fusible adhesive by Therm O Web.*

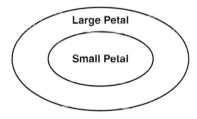

Lettering

Cherish the Moment Journal Templates

Pearl Needlework Set

Designs by Karen Neary

This three-piece set is a delight to sew. Quilting and sewing friends will appreciate your thoughtfulness when they receive this gift from you. And who knows, maybe you'll find time to make a set for yourself too!

Estimated Time
4 hours

Needlework Set

Finished sizes
Chatelaine: 2¼ x 42 inches
Pincushion: approximately
3 inches in diameter
Needle Case: approximately 3 inches in diameter

Materials
- Lightweight woven 44/45-inch-wide cotton/ metallic fabric:
    1 fat quarter main color*
    1 fat quarter contrast fabric A*
    1 fat quarter contrast fabric B*
- 8 x 8-inch square stiff interfacing
- 2¾ x 42½ inches lightweight batting
- 4 x 1½ inches white felt
- Small amount polyester fiberfill
- 5 (¼-inch) pearl shank buttons
- 1 (¼-inch) clear nylon snap fastener
- Basic sewing supplies and equipment

*Fairy Frost flamingo (MC), cameo (CC) and mango (CC) from Michael Miller Fabrics were used for model project.

Chatelaine

Cutting
From main color fabric:
- Cut two 2¾ x 18-inch strips for front.

From contrast fabric A:
- Cut two 2¾ x 21½-inch strips for backing.
- Cut one 22 x 1½-inch strip for scissors holder.
- Cut one 2¾ x 2¾-inch square for plain block.
- Use template provided to cut two pentagons for flowers.

From contrast fabric B:
- Use template provided (page 117) to cut one pentagon for flower.

Piecing

Use ¼-inch-wide seam allowances.

1. Sew front strips together to make a 35½-inch-long strip. Cut 2¾ x 2¾-inch square from each end of joined strip. Reserve squares for step 3.

2. Copy pinwheel pattern three times. Use copies to foundation-piece three Pinwheel blocks with contrast fabrics A and B. Remove paper foundations.

3. Sew one Pinwheel block to end of front strip. Sew reserved square from step 1 to Pinwheel blocks at each end of strip.

4. Measure and cut across strip 2½ inches from the Pinwheel blocks on each end of the front strip (Figure 1a). On one end of strip, sew plain block cut from first contrast fabric. On opposite end, sew remaining Pinwheel block. Sew the cutoff lengths back onto the ends of the front strip (Figure 1b).

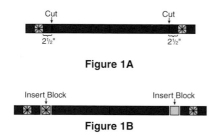

Figure 1A

Figure 1B

Assembly

Use ¼-inch wide seam allowances.

1. Fold 22 x 1½-inch strip for scissors tie in half lengthwise with right sides together. Sew long edges together. Turn right side out and press. Tie a knot in each end.

2. Fold scissors tie in half. On right side of front strip, with fold even with raw edge, stitch scissors tie to end of strip with two Pinwheel blocks.

3. Sew backing pieces together. Layer front strip and backing strip with right sides together. Layer batting onto wrong side of backing. Stitch around outer edges through all thicknesses, leaving an

8-inch opening for turning. Turn to right side, press and hand-stitch opening closed.

4. For flowers, press raw edges of pentagon shapes under ⅛ inch. Run a machine gathering stitch ¼ inch from folded edges and pull up stitches to gather.

5. Hand-sew flower over Pinwheel blocks, attaching pearl buttons in centers.

Needle Case

Cutting

From main-color fabric:
• Use pentagon template to cut two pieces on fold (Figure 2).

Figure 2

From contrast fabric B:
• Use pentagon template to cut one piece for flower.

From stiff interfacing:
• Use template provided to cut one pentagon on fold, less ¼-inch seam allowance all around.

Assembly

Use ¼-inch-wide seam allowances.

1. Center 4 x 1½-inch piece of white felt on the right side of one pentagon piece. Stitch across center of felt.

2. Sew both pentagon pieces with right sides together, leaving one side open. Turn right side out and press.

3. Slip Timtex pentagon piece inside needle case; hand-stitch side opening closed.

4. Sew snap fastener to inside at point.

5. Assemble flower as in step 4 of Chatelaine, Assembly. Hand-stitch to top of needle case, attaching pearl button in center of flower.

Pincushion

Cutting

From main-color fabric:
• Use pentagon template to cut two pieces for top and bottom.

From contrast fabric B:
• Use pentagon template to cut one piece for flower.

Assembly

Use ¼-inch-wide seam allowances.

1. Sew top and bottom pieces with right sides together, leaving an opening for turning. Turn right side out. Press.

2. Stuff lightly with polyester fiberfill. Hand-stitch opening closed.

3. Assemble flower as in step 4 of Chatelaine, Assembly. Hand-stitch to pincushion through top and bottom, attaching pearl button in center of flower. ⏱

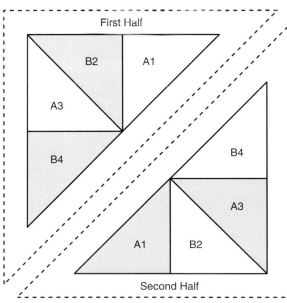

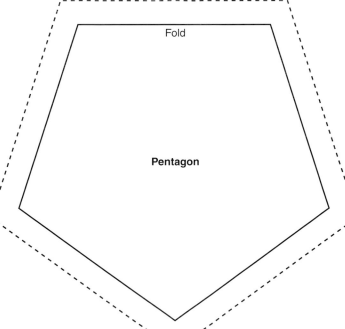

Pearl Needlework Set Template

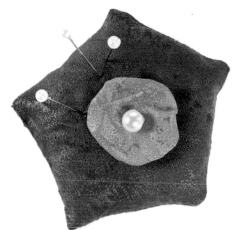

Pinwheel Foundation-Piecing Template

Pinwheel Piecing

Note: Attach block pieces in the numerical order indicated on pattern.

1. Cut an A1 piece large enough to cover the A1 pattern section plus ¼-inch seam allowance all around. Place fabric piece on the back of the foundation paper with the wrong side of the fabric facing the back of the foundation paper (Figure 1), taking care to watch the grain line of the fabric. *Note: Hold the paper up to a light source to check for proper placement. If desired, hold fabric in place with a dab of glue from a glue stick.*

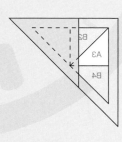

Figure 1

2. Cut a B2 piece of fabric large enough to cover the B2 pattern section plus ¼-inch seam allowance all around. Place fabric piece on wrong side of foundation square with the right side of piece B2 on top of the right side of piece A1 and the ¼-inch seam allowance extending into B2 pattern section (Figure 2).

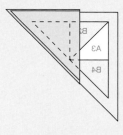

Figure 2

3. Carefully turn the foundation paper over so the marked side of the paper is facing you, taking care not to move the fabric pieces just placed. Sew on the line of the paper foundation pattern that divides pieces A1 and B2 (Figure 3).

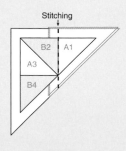

Figure 3

4. Fold fabric piece B2 over the seam just sewn and check placement by holding up to a light source. The pattern section should be totally covered by the fabric piece with the ¼-inch seam allowance on all sides (Figure 4).

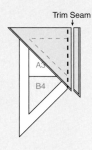

Figure 4

5. With the printed side of the foundation pattern facing upwards, fold the foundation paper on the seam line just sewn so that the printed sides of that paper are facing each other and the seam allowance of fabric pieces A1 and B2 is exposed (Figure 5). Trim the seam allowance to ⅛ inch using a rotary cutter and mat.

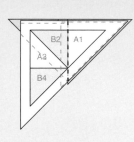

Figure 5

6. Unfold foundation paper and press fabric B2 into position, flattening the fold line in the foundation paper at the same time (Figure 6).

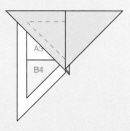

Figure 6

Repeat steps 2–6 to attach fabric pieces A3 and B4 to the foundation paper pattern. Press. Trim edges, leaving ¼-inch seam allowance on all sides.

Follow the same process to piece together the second half of the block. Sew halves together on center diagonal line. Remove foundation paper. Use a straight pin to remove paper between stitches as needed.

Sew Fun
Sewing Basket

Designs by Chris Malone

Nothing gives more pleasure than a thoughtful gift made by hand. Use a purchased basket, add your own personal style with your fabric choices and give to your sewing friends.

Estimated Time
4 hours

Sewing Basket Set

Finished size
Sewing Basket: varies
Pin Cushion: 4¾ x 4¾ inches

Materials
• Basket with handle and straight sides*
• 44/45-inch-wide woven fabric:
    ¾ yard black-with-white print for lining and pincushion
    ⅓ yard black-and-white check for ruffle
    ⅛ yard green print for leaves
• Scraps red, black and white prints for yo-yo flowers and pincushion center
• Ribbon:
    1 yard ¼-inch-wide black-and-white check
    1 yard ⅜-inch-wide red dot
    1 yard 1⅜-inch-wide wire-edged black-and-white check
• Buttons:
    4 (¾-inch) white
    2 (⅝-inch) white
    3 (⅜-inch) black and/or white round with shank
• 72 white E beads
• Small piece batting to fit bottom of basket

• Polyester fiberfill
• Black or white #8 pearl cotton
• Black or white beading or quilting thread
• Cardboard to fit bottom of basket
• Permanent fabric adhesive
• Pair of sewing scissors
• Basic sewing supplies and equipment

Model is 6½ inches high, with a 36-inch circumference.

Project Note: *To gather, set machine to an open zigzag stitch. Lay pearl cotton over stitching line and sew over the cord, taking care not to catch the cord in the stitching. Pull cord ends to gather.*

Measure Basket

1. Measure inside height of basket (A).

2. Measure circumference of basket around rim (B).

3. Place pattern tracing paper or tissue paper in bottom of basket and draw around edges to make pattern for padded basket bottom.

Cutting

From cardboard:
• Use pattern for padded bottom to cut one piece.

From batting:
• Use pattern for padded bottom to cut one piece.

From black-with-white print for lining and pincushion:
• Cut a piece(s) the height of the basket (A) plus 2½ inches, by twice the circumference measurement (B) for lining.
• Cut one piece approximately 2 inches larger all around than pattern for padded basket bottom for lining bottom.
• Cut two 2 x 2-inch squares and two 2 x 5-inch rectangles for pincushion top.
• Cut one 5 x 5-inch square for pincushion bottom.

From black-and-white check for ruffle:
• Cut a strip(s) 5 inches wide by twice the circumference measurement (B).

From scraps red, black and white prints for yo-yo flowers and pincushion center:
• Cut three 5-inch-diameter and three 3½-inch-diameter circles for yo-yo flowers.
• Cut one 2 x 2-inch square for pincushion center.

Pincushion Assembly

Use ¼-inch-wide seam allowances unless otherwise stated. Sew pieces with right sides together.

1. Sew two black-and-white 2 x 2-inch squares to opposite sides of the 2 x 2-inch square for pincushion center. Press seams outward.

2. Sew one 2 x 5-inch rectangle to each side of joined squares to make pincushion top. Press seams outward.

3. Sew pincushion top and bottom together, leaving a 2-inch opening along one side for turning. Trim corners and turn right side out. Stuff pincushion firmly with polyester fiberfill. Fold in seam allowance and stitch opening closed.

4. Sew beads around edge of pincushion, using approximately 15 on each side. Set pincushion aside.

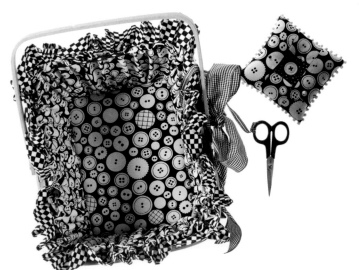

Sewing Basket Assembly

Use ¼-inch-wide seam allowances unless otherwise stated. Sew pieces with right sides together.

1. Seam strips for ruffle as needed to achieve total length. Sew short ends of joined strips together to form a tube. Fold ruffle in half lengthwise with wrong sides together. Press.

2. Referring to Project Note, stitch ½ inch from raw edge and gather to fit inside basket, leaving slightly loose. Tie gathering threads together and clip excess thread. Adjust gathers evenly around ruffle.

3. Apply adhesive to a few inches along gathering line of ruffle and press onto inside edge of basket, allowing ruffle to extend 1¾ inches above top edge of basket. Continue applying adhesive and pressing ruffle to attach entire ruffle.

4. Sew short edges of lining together to form a tube. Fold down a 1¼-inch hem along one edge. Press. Gather top and bottom of lining in same manner as for ruffle, stitching 1 inch from the top folded edge and ½ inch from the bottom raw edge.

5. Glue top of lining inside basket as for ruffle, placing so top of lining is 1¼ inches below top of ruffle. Working a small section at a time, apply adhesive to bottom inside edge of basket and pull lining straight down, pressing the gathering line onto the adhesive.

6. Glue batting to cardboard bottom piece. Hand-stitch long gathering stitches around edge of basket-bottom lining fabric. Place fabric wrong side up on work surface. Place a small amount of polyester fiberfill in center of fabric; place batting/cardboard, batting side down, over polyfill. Pull stitches to gather fabric snugly over the edge. Reinforce with dots of adhesive. Apply adhesive in bottom of basket. Insert padded bottom and press down firmly.

7. Beginning at the inside center back of basket, glue the red-dot ribbon over the gather line of lining, overlapping ends. Using black pearl cotton, sew through one ¾-inch white button; glue button over ends of ribbon.

8. Fold ¼-inch-wide black-and-white-check ribbon in half, forming a small loop at fold. Sew a ¾-inch white button to ribbon to secure loop. Glue button inside center front of basket opposite first button (Figure 1). Tack one end of ribbon to center back of pincushion. Sew a ¾-inch white button to center of pincushion on front and back, covering the ribbon end and pulling thread to indent center. Tie opposite end of ribbon around handle of sewing scissors.

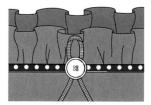

Figure 1

9. To make yo-yo flowers, hand-stitch edge of each 5-inch circle using a double strand of matching thread. Pull tightly to gather. Smooth and flatten with opening in the center. Gather 3½-inch circles in same manner, turning edge under ⅛ inch before stitching. Sew remaining E beads around edge of one small yo-yo flower. Layer large and small yo-yos with opening on back of large yo-yos and on the front of small yo-yos. Sew a shank button to the center of each flower.

10. Fold green print fabric for leaves in half with right sides facing. Trace leaf pattern five times and stitch on traced lines, leaving bottoms open. Cut out ⅛ inch from stitching. Trim tip and turn right side out. Turn bottom raw edges under ¼ inch. Press. Whipstitch bottom edges together and fold in a pleat at bottom; tack to hold (Figure 2).

11. Arrange yo-yo flowers and leaves on front of basket and glue in place. Tie 1⅜-inch-wide black-and-white-check ribbon in a bow around basket handle. Loop ribbon tails on each side of bow, folding at midway. Sew a ⅝-inch white button to each fold using black pearl cotton; glue fold to basket rim. ☼

Source: Fabri-Tac permanent fabric adhesive from Beacon Adhesives Inc.

Quick Tip

Glue is sometimes the quickest, easiest and strongest choice for joining fabric pieces, even for those of us that love to sew. The key is to choose the adhesive most appropriate for the task, apply it carefully and neatly and allow enough time for the glue to set before going on to the next step.

Figure 2

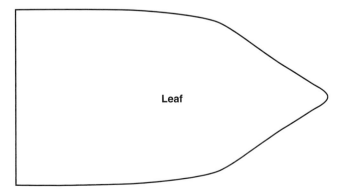

Leaf

Sew Fun Sewing Basket Template

Porcelain Pincushion

Design by Chris Malone

Invite your sewing friends over for an afternoon tea and sewing party. They'll be surprised when you give them this pretty, simple-to-sew pincushion made from a teacup and saucer.

Estimated Time
2½ hours

Pincushion

Finished size
5⅞ x 3¼ inches

Materials
- Teacup and matching saucer with pink roses pattern
- ¼ yard 44/45-inch-wide pink rose-print fabric
- Simulated white pearl beads:
    approximately 102 (3mm)
    approximately 20 (5mm)
- Ribbon:
    30 inches ⅞-inch-wide pink wire-edged
    20 inches ⅝-inch-wide green wire-edged
    12 inches ⅜-inch-wide white sheer
- 3 (2–3-inch-long) needles (for pins)
- 3 assorted large glass beads (for pins)
- Polyester fiberfill
- White beading or quilting thread
- Beading or quilting needle
- Adhesives:
    permanent fabric
    glass/metal
    ceramics epoxy
- Basic sewing supplies and equipment

Ribbon Roses

1. Cut a 15-inch length of pink ribbon. Pull ¾ inch of wire from both sides of one end. Twist wires together to secure.

2. At the opposite end, carefully pull wire from one side of ribbon only until entire side is completely gathered and curling naturally. Do not clip wire.

3. To form rose, hold twisted end in one hand and begin to wrap gathered ribbon around itself with the other hand. Wrap tightly at first to form a bud; then wrap more loosely to shape and open rose as shown in photo. To end, fold the raw edge down

to meet the gathered edge. Twist the long wire around the short wires; clip the excess. ***Option:*** *Use needle and matching thread to make a few stitches to secure the wraps.* Use fingers to further shape and pinch the ribbon until desired look is achieved.

4. Repeat steps 1–3 to make a second rose.

Ribbon Leaves

1. Cut a 4-inch length of green ribbon. Fold length in half with ends even. Carefully pull the wire from the inner edges to gather ribbon (Figure 1).

Figure 1

2. Fold in excess ribbon at base of the leaf and wrap the exposed wires around it to hold the leaf shape (Figure 2). ***Option:*** *Use needle and matching thread to make a few stitches to hold the shape.* Use fingers to pinch a tip on the leaf.

Figure 2

3. Repeat steps 1 and 2 to make four more leaves.

Rosettes

1. Cut a 4-inch length of sheer white ribbon. Use a needle and matching thread to sew a gathering stitch as shown in Figure 3.

Figure 3

2. Pull thread to gather tightly. Overlap the ends and stitch them closed. Sew a small pearl in the center of the rosette.

3. Repeat steps 1 and 2 to make two more rosettes.

Instructions

1. Measure diameter of teacup at the top. Cut a circle from fabric 2½ times the teacup diameter. ***Note:*** *Model is 3⅝ inches in diameter. Fabric circle is 9 inches in diameter.*

2. Use double thread to hand-sew gathering stitches around the edge of the fabric circle or increase the stitch length and loosen the tension on your sewing machine to create a gathering stitch. After you sew the gathering stitch, place a ball of polyester polyfill in the center of the fabric on the wrong side and pull threads to gather fabric edges together. Keep adding polyfill until pincushion ball is full and firm and fits snugly in the cup. Knot and clip the thread.

3. Apply glass/metal adhesive to the inside of the cup, keeping adhesive away from the rim. Push the ball into place. ***Note:*** *Pincushion should extend above rim of cup about 1¼ inches.* Let dry.

4. Thread a beading or quilting needle with 2 strands of beading or quilting thread. Start the needle in the pincushion just above the rim at the side where the handle is attached. Pick up pearl beads—three small, one large and three more small—then insert needle back into pincushion about ⅝ inch from first stitch, leaving a shallow loop as an edging. Bring needle back out ⅛ inch away and repeat bead sequence. Continue around edge of pincushion (Figure 4).

Figure 4

5. Glue teacup to saucer with ceramics epoxy following manufacturer's instructions. Let dry completely.

6. Referring to photo for placement, use permanent fabric adhesive to glue one ribbon rose onto pincushion near cup handle, with two leaves and two rosettes on one side of the rose and one leaf and the third rosette on the other side. Glue the second rose to the base of the teacup with a leaf tucked under each side.

7. Use glass/metal adhesive to glue a glass bead to the end of each long needle to make decorative pins. Let dry. Insert pins in pincushion. ⏱

Sources: Fabri-Tac and Glass, Metal & More adhesives from Beacon Adhesives Inc.

Quick Tip

For a similar gift for a less "fancy" friend, make a pincushion using a sturdy mug and whimsical fabric. Embellish it with a fun trim instead of pearls and ribbon roses.

Dynamic Home Decor

Your home is an extended expression of your unique sense of style. By using your signature color palette, rich decorator fabric, and to-die-for trim, you'll add style to your home and save money and time. And remember, you can add dynamic style with these projects in a weekend or less.

One-Step-Up Footstool

Design by Carol Zentgraf

Make an upholstered footstool to coordinate with the decor of any room. It's easy when you begin with a basic wooden footstool.

Estimated Time
3 hours

Footstool

Finished size
15¼ x 15¾ x 11¾ inches

Materials
- 11 x 15 x 10-inch-high wooden footstool
- 9 large scraps medium- heavyweight decorator fabrics
- 1½ yards 6-inch-long bullion fringe
- 1½ yards trim with decorative header
- 1 (11 x 15-inch) rectangle 4-inch-thick upholstery foam
- 23 x 27-inch rectangle high-loft batting
- 4 (1-inch) cover-button forms
- 4 (1-inch) 2-hole buttons
- 6-inch upholstery needle
- Waxed button thread
- Electric drill with ¼-inch bit
- Staple gun
- Permanent fabric adhesive
- Basic sewing supplies and equipment

Cutting
Note: *Refer to Figure 1, Assembly Diagram on page 130.*

From decorator fabric scraps:
- Cut one 5 x 6-inch rectangle for center block (E).
- Cut two 6 x 11-inch rectangles for center of two sides (B and H).
- Cut two 5 x 11-inch rectangles for center of two sides (D and F).
- Cut four 11 x 11-inch squares for corners (A, C, G and I).

A	B	C
D	E	F
G	H	I

Figure 1
Assembly Diagram

Assembly

Use ½-inch-wide seam allowances throughout.

1. Sew long edges of A, B and C together to make the top row. Repeat with G, H and I to make the bottom row. Sew one short edge of D to a short edge of E. Sew one short edge of F to the opposite short edge of E. Sew the rows together, matching seams; press.

2. On the top of the footstool, draw a line 3½ inches from each long edge. Draw a line 5 inches from each short edge. The resulting center rectangle should measure 4 x 5 inches. Drill a hole at the intersections of the lines (Figure 2).

Figure 2

3. Using permanent fabric adhesive, glue upholstery foam rectangle to the top of the stool. Center the batting on the foam. Wrap the batting around the foam and the stool top, pulling tightly, and staple the batting to the underside of the stool top (Figure 3). Trim excess batting.

Underside of Top

Figure 3

4. With the right side up, center the pieced cover on the foam. Pin around the edges to secure.

5. Cover buttons with decorator fabric, following manufacturer's instructions. Cut an 18-inch length of waxed button thread and slide the shank of one covered button onto the center of the thread. Insert both ends of the thread through the eye of the upholstery needle.

6. At one corner of the center panel (E) of the cover, insert the upholstery needle straight through the foam (Figure 4). Pull needle out of the corresponding drilled hole in the top of the footstool (Figure 5). Pull the thread ends completely through the drilled hole and button, and insert needle through remaining hole of the two-hole button (Figure 6). Remove needle and pull thread tightly to create a tuft in the cushion; then knot the thread ends securely. Repeat at each remaining corner of the center block.

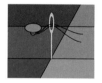

Figure 4   **Figure 5**   **Figure 6**

7. Remove pins from the sides of the cover. Pull cover edges tautly to the underside of the footstool and staple in place. Trim excess fabric.

8. Glue bullion fringe around the edges of the footstool. Glue trim with decorative header on top of bullion fringe upper edge. ⏱

Sources: Deluxe Collection fabric from Waverly Fabrics; bullion trim and tassel trim from Expo International; Nu-Foam upholstery foam alternative and Poly-fil Hi-loft batting from Fairfield Processing Corp.; cover buttons, upholstery needle and waxed button thread from Prym Consumer USA; Fabri-Tac permanent fabric adhesive from Beacon Adhesives.

Simply Striped
Pillow Trio

Designs by Carol Zentgraf

Get creative with striped fabric by piecing it into interesting effects. It's all in the cutting! Be sure the stripe is evenly repeated for the inside or outside angle designs.

Estimated Time
2 hours
Per Pillow

Center Cross Pillow

Finished size
18 x 18 inches

Materials
• 1 yard 54-inch-wide striped decorator fabric
• Scraps coordinating decorator fabric for covered buttons
• Self-adhesive, double-sided basting tape
• 18 x 18-inch square pillow form
• 2 (1¾-inch) square cover-button forms
• Waxed button thread
• Upholstery needle
• Basic sewing supplies and equipment

Template
Draw a square on tracing or pattern paper as indicate in cutting instructions. Draw diagonal lines from corner to corner, creating four triangles. Add ½-inch-wide seam allowances to the sides of one triangle and cut out for cutting template (Figure 1).

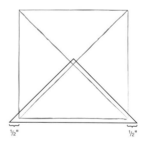

½"   ½"

Figure 1

Cutting
Make triangle template from a 19-inch square.

From stripe decorator fabric:
• Place triangle template on fabric with the base of the triangle running perpendicular to the stripes, centering the triangle on a stripe (Figure 2 on page 134). Cut out the triangle. Reposition the template in the same manner and cut out three more triangles.

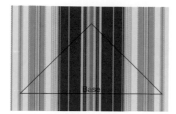

Figure 2

• Cut one 19 x 19-inch square for pillow back.

Assembly

Use ½-inch-wide seam allowances. Sew right sides together.

1. To assemble front panel, baste the sides of two triangles together with basting tape, making sure the stripes are aligned. Sew together and press seams. Repeat for remaining two triangles. Baste the two sets of triangles together along long edges, matching stripes; sew together and press.

2. Sew pieced front to back, leaving one side open. Turn right side out and press, pressing under seam allowance of opening.

3. Insert pillow form. Slipstitch opening closed.

4. Cover buttons with scraps of decorator fabric following manufacturer's instructions. Cut an 18-inch length of waxed button thread and slide the shank of one button onto the center of the thread. Insert both thread ends through the eye of the upholstery needle.

5. Stitch through the center of the pillow and out the center back. Remove the needle and tie the thread ends through the shank of the remaining button, pulling tightly to tuft the center of the pillow. Knot the thread ends securely and cut excess thread ends.

Center Square Pillow

Finished size

16 x 16 inches

Materials

• 1 yard 54-inch-wide stripe decorator fabric
• 2 yards tassel trim with decorative header
• Self-adhesive, double-sided basting tape
• 16 x 16-inch square pillow form
• Permanent fabric adhesive
• Basic sewing supplies and equipment

Cutting

Make triangle template from a 17-inch square adding ½-inch-wide seam allowances (Figure 1, page 132).

From stripe decorator fabric:

• Place template on fabric with the base of the triangle running parallel to the stripes (Figure 3). Cut out the triangle. Reposition the template in the same manner and cut out three more triangles.

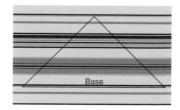

Figure 3

• Cut one 17 x 17-inch square for pillow back.

Assembly

Use ½-inch-wide seam allowances. Sew right sides together.

1. Repeat steps 1–3 of Center Cross Pillow Assembly.

2. Glue tassel trim around edges of pillow using permanent fabric adhesive.

Striped Side Border Pillow

Finished size

12 x 19 inches

Materials

- 54-inch-wide decorator fabric:
  - ½ yard floral
  - ¾ yard stripe
- 12 x 16-inch pillow form
- 2 (1⅝-inch) square cover-button forms with frames
- Basic sewing supplies and equipment

Cutting

From floral decorator fabric:
- Cut two 13 x 17-inch rectangles for front and back.

From striped decorator fabric:
- Cut one 7 x 25-inch strip along the length of the stripes for border strip.

Assembly

Use ½-inch-wide seam allowances. Sew right sides together.

1. Sew pillow front to back along both long edges and one short edge. Turn right side out. Press.

2. Sew short edges of border strip together. Press in half with wrong sides together.

3. Slip border strip over pillow front and back with raw edges even, aligning seams (Figure 4). Serge edges together, or sew and finish raw edges.

Figure 4

4. Press seam allowance toward floral fabric. Topstitch ¼ inch from seam line, catching seam allowances in stitching.

5. Insert pillow form in cover. Tack borders together in center.

6. Following manufacturer's instructions, cover buttons with scraps of floral decorator fabric and add the frames. Hand-sew a button to each side of the border center, covering the tack stitching. ⏱

Sources: *Santa Cruz and Bastille fabrics from Thibaut Fabrics; tassel trim from Expo International; Wonder Tape basting tape from Prym Consumer USA; Fabri-Tac permanent fabric adhesive from Beacon Adhesives.*

"What in the World" Table-Panel Shower Curtain

Design by Carol Zentgraf

Transform a pretty printed tablecloth panel into a shower curtain with the simple addition of coordinating borders and curtain grommets.

Estimated Time
3 hours

Panel

Finished size
72 x 72 inches

Materials
• 70 x 70-inch square tablecloth panel
• 2⅛ yards 54-inch-wide coordinating check decorator fabric
• 2⅛ yards 18-inch-wide fusible interfacing
• 12 (1⁹⁄₁₆-inch) snap-together curtain grommets
• Basic sewing supplies and equipment

Cutting
From coordinating check decorator fabric:
• Cut two 3 x 70-inch lengthwise strips for side borders.
• Cut one 9 x 73-inch strip for top border.

From interfacing:
• Cut one 9 x 73-inch strip.

Assembly
Use ¼-inch-wide seam allowances. Sew right sides together.

1. Fuse the interfacing to the wrong side of the top border strip following manufacturer's instructions.

2. Press side border strips in half lengthwise with wrong sides together to make a center crease. Open strips. With right sides together, sew one long edge of each strip to a side edge of the tablecloth panel. Press seam allowances toward border strips.

3. Finish raw edges of border strips with serger or zigzag stitches. Fold border strips to the wrong side of the tablecloth panel along the pressed center crease with the finished edge of the border strips overlapping the seam. Pin in place. From the right side of the tablecloth, topstitch along the border seam, securing the back edges in the stitching.

4. Press short edges of top border under ½ inch. Repeat steps 2 and 3 to sew top border to top edge of tablecloth panel. Topstitch short edges together at each end.

5. Place curtain on a large flat surface. Evenly space the curtain grommets along the center of the top border and mark centers. Follow manufacturer's instructions to attach grommets.

6. Press the lower edge of the curtain under in a doubled 1-inch hem. Topstitch in place. ⏱

Source: *French Toile tablecloth panel and French check fabric from French Connections; Dritz Home curtain grommets from Prym Consumer USA.*

Flowers & Stripes
Tablecloth

Designs by Carol Zentgraf

Pick a floral home-decor fabric and accent it with a strong stripe fabric to create this luxurious table top. Finish with matching napkins for a designer look. But keep your secret to yourself; there's no need to let anyone know you did this in a weekend.

Estimated Time
3 hours

Tablecloth

Finished sizes
Tablecloth: 60 x 84 inches
Napkin: 20 x 20 inches
Napkin Ring: 2 inches wide x 2 inches in diameter

Materials
• 44-inch-wide cotton fabric:
    3½ yards floral print
    2½ yards coordinating stripe
• 4 (1-inch-diameter) cover-button form
• 18 inch ruler
• Basic sewing supplies and equipment

Cutting
From floral print:
• Cut one 43 x 67-inch rectangle for tablecloth center panel.
• Cut four 22 x 22-inch squares for napkins.
• Cut four scraps of fabric to cover buttons for napkin rings.

From coordinating stripe:
• Cut eight 10½-inch strips across the width of the fabric.
• Cut four 5 x 8-inch strips for napkin rings.

Assembly

Use ½-inch-wide seam allowances. Sew right sides together.

1. Sew short edges of stripe strips together, matching stripes, to make four 88-inch strips. Press seam allowances open. Fold each stripe strip in half, using the center seam as the guide. Cut two strips to 86 inches long and two to 62 inches long for border strips by removing length from outside strips.

2. Mark the center of each side of the center panel. Pin border strips to corresponding edges, matching center marks to border center seams. Sew border strips to center panel, stitching to ½ inch from each corner.

3. To miter border strips at each corner, fold the corner in half with right sides together and adjacent border strips even. Pin the loose ends of the strips together. With 18 inch ruler aligned with the fold, draw a line from the end of the stitching to the corner of the border strips (Figure 1). Pin strips together along the line. Stitch along the line and trim excess corner fabric. Press seams open.

Figure 1

4. Press tablecloth edges under in a ½-inch double hem. Topstitch in place ⅜ inch from the outside edge.

5. On opposite edges of 22 x 22-inch square for napkin, press under a doubled ½-inch hem and topstitch. Repeat for remaining edges. Repeat for remaining napkins.

6. To make napkin ring, fold 5 x 8-inch stripe strip in half lengthwise with right sides together. Sew long edges and one short edge together. Trim seam allowance. Turn right side out and press. Press raw open edge under. Edgestitch around all edges.

7. Cover button with scrap of floral print fabric following manufacturer's instructions. Overlap ends of strip 1 inch. Sew button in place through strip ends to secure. Repeat for remaining napkin rings. ⏱

Source: *Wainscott fabric collection from Windham Fabrics.*

Trapunto
Table Topper

Design by Carol Zentgraf

Create an elegant topper for your table when you use free-motion quilting to outline the fabric design.

Estimated Time
4 hours

Table Topper

Finished size
53 x 53 inches

Materials
- 54-inch-wide decorator fabric:
    - 1⅝ yards floral print
    - 1⅝ yards coordinating stripe
- High-loft batting
- Free-motion sewing-machine foot
- Basic sewing supplies and equipment

Cutting
From floral print fabric:
- Cut one 54 x 54-inch square.

From coordinating stripe fabric:
- Cut one 54 x 54-inch square.

From high-loft batting:
- Cut one 54 x 54-inch square.

Assembly
Use ½-inch-wide seam allowances.

1. Layer fabric with right sides together and batting on top, aligning edges. Sew together, leaving an opening for turning.

2. Turn right side out. Press under opening seam allowance. Slipstitch opening closed.

3. Place topper on flat surface with floral side up. Pin topper layers together around selected motifs.

4. Attach free-motion sewing-machine foot or darning foot. Using matching thread, stitch around each motif, stitching along motif edge or slightly beyond, as desired. Refer to your owner's manual to set your machine for free-motion sewing. ⏱

Sources: Summer Splendor and Serene Stripe fabric from Waverly Fabrics; Poly-fil high-loft batting from Fairfield Processing Corp.

Just-Like-New
Seat Cushions

Design by Carol Zentgraf

Complement your quilted table topper with chair cushions that showcase the same technique.

Estimated Time
3 hours

Seat Cushions

Finished size
Custom fitted

Materials
- 54-inch-wide decorator fabric:
    floral print for cushion top
    coordinating print for cushion bottom
       and boxing strip
    coordinating solid for piping
- ¼-inch cord
- Muslin
- High-loft batting
- 2-inch-thick upholstery foam
- 1 yard 1½-inch-wide coordinating grosgrain ribbon
- Permanent fabric adhesive
- Permanent marker
- Heavy-duty scissors
- Free-motion sewing-machine foot
- Basic sewing supplies and equipment

Preparation

1. Place pattern tracing paper on chair seat and draw pattern for cushion. Add ½ inch all around for seam allowance. Cut out pattern. Measure pattern length and width to determine yardage for cushion top and bottom.

2. For the boxing strip, measure the perimeter of the pattern and add 1 inch. Fabric will need to be this length by 3 inches wide.

3. Multiply the pattern perimeter by 2 and add 6 inches to determine the length of the cord. Allow ½ yard of fabric to cover cord.

Cutting

From floral print fabric for cushion top:
• Use cushion pattern to cut one top.

From coordinating print fabric for cushion bottom and boxing strip:
• Use cushion pattern to cut one bottom.
• Cut one 3-inch-wide strip by the length determined in step 2 of Preparation.

From coordinating solid fabric for piping:
• Cut 1½-inch-wide bias strips the width of the fabric. Sew short ends together to equal length of cord determined in step 3 of Preparation.

From muslin:
• Use cushion pattern to cut one piece.

From batting:
• Use cushion pattern to cut one piece.

From upholstery foam:
• Trim seam allowance from cushion pattern. Draw around outline with permanent marker. Cut out cushion using heavy-duty scissors and cutting in layers, being careful to keep edges perpendicular to the top and bottom.

Assembly

1. Layer batting between muslin and wrong side of cushion top. Align edges and pin together. Select motifs to be quilted and pin layers together around each motif. Using free-motion sewing-machine or darning foot, stitch around motifs with matching thread. Refer to your owner's manual to set your machine for free-motion sewing.

2. Cover cord with bias binding to make piping. Beginning at center back of cushion, with piping ½ inch from edge, stitch piping to cushion top using a zipper or cording foot. Sew piping to cushion bottom in same manner.

3. Using a ½-inch seam, sew short edges of boxing strip together. With right sides together, sew one edge of boxing strip to edge of top cushion. Repeat by sewing remaining edge to bottom cushion, leaving back edge open to insert foam.

4. Cover foam cushion with one or two layers of batting, gluing edges in place with permanent fabric adhesive. Insert cushion in cover. If desired, add additional batting to fill out cover. Slipstitch opening edge closed.

5. Cut ribbon length in half for ties. Place cushion on chair and mark location for ties. Hand-stitch center of a ribbon length to each marked tie position. ⏱

Sources: *Nu-Foam Upholstery Alternative and Poly-fil high-loft batting from Fairfield Processing Corp.; Fabri-Tac permanent adhesive from Beacon Adhesives.*

Fat-Quarter Duvet Cover

Design by Carol Zentgraf

A duvet cover is a great way to dress your home office for over night guests. This quick and easy duvet cover features fabrics from two colorways of the same fat quater collection.

Estimated Time
6 hours

Duvet Cover

Finished size
72 x 93½ inches

Materials
- 27 cotton print fat quarters
- 6 yards 44/45-inch-wide coordinating cotton print fabric for backing
- 4 yards 1–1½-inch-wide ribbon
- Basic sewing supplies and equipment

Cutting

From 27 cotton print fat quarters:
- Cut four 8½ x 8½-inch squares from each print for a total of 108 squares.

From 6 yards coordinating cotton print fabric:
- Cut yardage in half to make two 108-inch lengths the width of the fabric for backing.

From ribbon:
- Cut 10 (14-inch) lengths for ties.

Assembly

Use ¼-inch-wide seam allowances through-out. Sew with right sides together unless otherwise stated.

1. Sew squares together in 12 rows of nine blocks each. Press. Sew rows together, matching seams of blocks. Press.

2. Sew backing fabric pieces together along long edge using a ½-inch-wide seam allowance. Press seam allowance open. Trim backing to fit pieced top.

3. Sew top and backing together along sides and lower edge using a ½-inch-wide seam allowance. Turn right side out. Press.

4. Press upper edges of duvet cover under in a double 1½-inch hem and pin in place.

5. Beginning 2 inches from each side of the top of duvet cover, insert 1 inch of a ribbon tie under folded hem. Fold ribbon up over the hem and pin in place (Figure 1). Repeat across hemmed edge, spacing three more ribbon ties evenly across. Add the remaining five ribbon ties in the same manner on the bottom side to correspond with the first five ties.

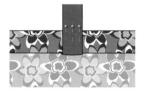

Figure 1

6. With the folded hem side up, stitch close to each edge of the hem, securing both the hem and the ties. ⏱

Source: Modern Grace fat quarters collection from Windham Fabrics.

Quick Tip

To make the corners of your squares nest together neatly, press seam allowances of the rows in alternating directions before sewing the rows together.

Hideaway
Shelving Unit

Design by Pamela Hastings

Create hidden storage for your home office supplies that will double as a side table or nightstand. An inexpensive shelving unit and a few yards of fabric can conquer your clutter in no time.

Estimated Time
5 hours

Shelving Unit

Finished size
Custom fit

Materials
- Assembled 3-shelf wire or plastic shelving unit
- 54-inch-wide decorator fabric:
    2 yards floral print for body of cover
    1¾ yards contrasting print for shelf topper
- 1-inch-wide half sew-on/half self-adhesive hook-and-loop tape
- Basic sewing supplies and equipment

Cutting
From fabric for body of cover:
- Beginning at front edge of shelf unit, measure across short side, around the back and across the opposite short side as shown. Add 4 inches to this measurement for fabric width. Measure the height of the shelf unit and add 4 inches for fabric length (Figure 1). Cut fabric for body of cover to these dimensions for side/back panel.

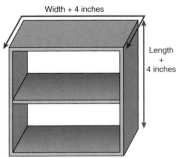

Figure 1

• For removable front panel, measure the width and height of the front of the shelf unit. Add 1 inch to both the height and width measurements. Cut two fabric rectangles for the front panel.

From contrasting fabric for shelf topper:
• Measure the width and length of the top of the shelf unit. Add 1 inch to both width and length measurement. Cut two shelf top pieces to these dimensions.
• Using the length from the cut shelf topper, cut four topper front/back panels this length by 7 inches.
• Using the width from the cut shelf topper, cut four topper side panels this length by 7 inches.

Assembly

1. Sew a 1-inch double hem on all edges of side/back panel. Sew the sew-on half of hook-and-loop tape across the top edge of each panel, approximately ½ inch from the top.

2. Using a ½ inch seam allowance and with right sides together, sew the front panel on four sides, leaving a 5-inch opening for turning. Turn to right side. Slipstitch opening closed. Topstitch front panel. Sew hook-and-loop tape across the top edge of the pane, approximately ½ inch from the top.

3. With right sides together, sew each shelf topper side and topper front/back panels together, leaving top edges open. Trim corners, turn right side out and press (Figure 2).

Figure 2

4. Pin topper panels to the right side of one shelf top piece with raw edges even. Using a ½ inch seam allowance, machine-baste in place (Figure 3).

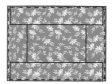

Figure 3

5. Leave topper panels on top of the shelf top piece. Pin remaining shelf topper panel to first panel, with right sides together and raw edges even. Stitch around edges using a ½-inch seam allowance and leaving a 5-inch opening on one side for turning.

6. Turn topper right side out and slipstitch opening closed (Figure 4).

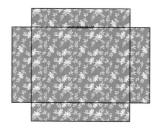

Figure 4

7. Attach adhesive side of hook-and-loop tape around all four sides of top of shelf unit. Attach side/back panel to tape around sides and back of shelf unit. Attach front panel to tape across front of unit.

8. Lay shelf topper over top of shelf unit. ○

Luxury Bath Ensemble

Designs by Agnes Mercik

Combine a print with a striped decorator fabric for a coordinating shower curtain and window treatment. The shower curtain is cut generously full for a luxurious look. Your sewing machine and serger team up to create these stylish pieces for the bath.

Estimated Time
5 hours

Bath Ensemble

Finished sizes

Shower Curtain With Attached Valance: 72 x 108 inches
Straight Window Valance: 50 x 18 inches
Puff Window Valance: 50 x 15 inches

Materials

- 54-inch-wide decorator fabrics:
    - 6½ yards print
    - 2 yards coordinating stripe
- ⅝ yard fusible interfacing
- 15 (1-inch) cover-button forms
- Permanent fabric adhesive
- Buttonhole cutter
- 1 (1-inch-wide) curtain rod for valance
- 1 (3-inch-wide) curtain rod for puff valance
- Basic sewing supplies and equipment

Shower Curtain With Attached Valance

Cutting

Measure shower and window openings.
Adjust dimensions accordingly.
Trim selvages from each fabric before cutting.
Cut strips across the fabric width unless otherwise indicated.

From print decorator fabric:
- Cut two 54 x 79-inch pieces for curtain.
- Cut two 8 x 54-inch pieces for valance.

From coordinating stripe decorator fabric:
- Cut two 17 x 54-inch pieces for valance trim.
- With the stripe running the length of each piece, cut 15 (6 x 8-inch) strips for rod tabs.

From fusible interfacing:
- Cut 15 (6 x 8-inch) strips for rod tabs.

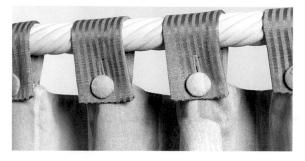

Assembly

Use a wide, medium-length, 4-thread serger stitch. If a 4-thread is not available, straight stitch a ⅜-inch-wide seam and edge finish with serging or zigzagging.

1. With right sides facing and long raw edges even, serge the 54 x 79-inch curtain pieces together.

2. Serge short ends of the 8 x 54-inch valance pieces together. Repeat with the 17 x 54-inch valance trim pieces. Press serged seams to one side.

3. Apply fusible interfacing strips to rod tab fabric strips following manufacturer's directions. Fold tabs in half lengthwise with right sides together and raw edges even. Serge long edges together. Fold serged seam allowance toward the strips; serge across one short end (Figure 1). Turn right side out and press.

Fold

Figure 1

4. Make 15 covered buttons using fabric circles cut from the decorator fabric as directed on the cover-button form package.

5. At serged end of each of the 15 tabs, make a vertical buttonhole to fit button. Apply a thin line of seam sealant on the wrong side of each buttonhole between the stitches and allow to dry. Cut buttonholes open. Set completed tabs aside.

6. With right sides together, stitch the striped valance strip to one long edge of the print valance strip. Press the seam toward the striped strip.

7. Turn under and press 1 inch at each long edge of the curtain panel. Turn under again and press to make a 1-inch-wide doubled hem. Machine-edgestitch or blind-stitch the hems in place. Hem the short edges of the print/striped valance panel in the same manner (Figure 2). ***Note:*** *When hemming heavier home decor fabrics, adjust the blind stitch for a deeper zigzag "bite" to ensure that the hem is securely stitched.*

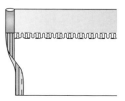

Figure 2

8. Turn under and press a 3-inch-wide double hem at the curtain lower edge. Stitch.

9. With the raw edges even, place a button tab right side down along the upper edge on the wrong side of the curtain panel just inside the inner finished edges of the side hems. Baste in place. Evenly space (about 5–6 inches apart) the remaining tabs and baste in place (Figure 3).

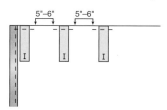

Figure 3

10. With wrong sides together and raw edges even, fold the valance strip in half. Pin the valance to the curtain panel with the print/striped half of the valance against the curtain wrong side and raw edges even. Serge the layers together. Turn the valance to the right side of the curtain and press. Edgestitch (Figure 4).

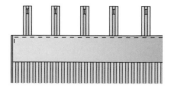

Figure 4

11. Fold the tabs down over the valance edge so the short finished edge is 1 inch below the upper edge of the curtain. Mark the button positions. Sew buttons in place, stitching securely through all fabric layers. Loop the tabs over the shower curtain rod and button in place.

Straight & Puff Window Valances

Cutting
Cut all strips across the fabric width.

From print fabric:
• Cut one 24 x 54-inch strip for puff valance.

From coordinating stripe fabric:
• Cut one 25 x 54-inch strip for straight valance.
• Cut one 7 x 54-inch strip for puff valance trim.

Assembly
1. Make a 1-inch-wide double hem at each short end of the 25 x 54-inch straight valance. Make a 2-inch-wide double hem at one long edge (see step 7 of Assembly for shower curtain). Make a 1-inch-wide double hem at the short ends of the 7 x 54-inch puff valance trim piece and the 24 x 54-inch puff valance piece.

2. Serge-finish the remaining long edge of the striped valance. Turn under and press 2½ inches to create a rod pocket. Machine-stitch in place through the center of the serging. Stitch again 1 inch from the upper pressed edge to create the ruffle (Figure 5).

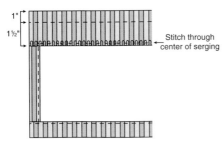

Figure 5

3. With wrong sides together and raw edges even, fold the 7 x 54-inch puff valance trim piece in half, matching long edges. Press. With wrong sides together and raw edges even, fold the 24 x 54-inch puff valance piece in half around the trim piece. Serge layers together (Figure 6).

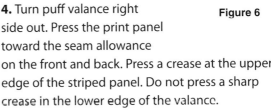

Figure 6

4. Turn puff valance right side out. Press the print panel toward the seam allowance on the front and back. Press a crease at the upper edge of the striped panel. Do not press a sharp crease in the lower edge of the valance.

5. Edgestitch along the upper creased edge. Slipstitch the print panel edges together for about ½ inch just below the seam line to enclose the raw edges of the serged seam (Figure 7).

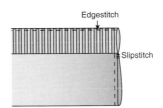

Figure 7

6. Slip the straight valance onto the 1-inch-wide curtain rod and the puff valance onto the 3-inch-wide curtain rod and hang on mounted hanging hardware. ⏱

Quick Tip

Make it easier to cover the buttons by machine basting ⅛ inch from the cut edges of each fabric circle. Pull the bobbin thread ends to gather the fabric around the button form. Tie off securely. For added security, add a dot of fabric glue to the knot and allow to dry before inserting the button back.

Monogrammed Bath Set

Designs by Carol Zentgraf

Dress up a bathroom vanity with this monogrammed tissue box cover, covered jewelry dish and reversible coaster.

Bath Set

Estimated Time
5 hours

Finished sizes
Tissue Cover: 5¾ x 6 x 5¾ inches
Jewelry Dish: 4¾ inches in diameter x 2¾ inches tall
Coaster: 4½ x 4½ inches

Materials
- 54-inch-wide decorator fabric:
    - ½ yard floral print
    - ½ yard coordinating patterned solid
- ½ yard stiff double-sided fusible interfacing
- 3¼ yards ½-inch-wide gimp
- ½ yard tassel trim with decorative header
- 2-inch-high and 4-inch-high machine-embroidery monogram designs
- Tear-away fabric stabilizer
- Rayon machine-embroidery thread
- Clear monofilament thread
- Permanent fabric adhesive
- Basic sewing supplies and equipment

Tissue Cover

Cutting
From floral print fabric:
- Cut two 6-inch squares for tissue cover top.
- Cut one 23½ x 6¼-inch rectangle for tissue cover liner.

From coordinating patterned solid fabric:
- Cut one 23½ x 6¼-inch rectangle for tissue cover sides. ***Note:** Depending on the size of hoop, embroidery may need to be done before cutting.*

From interfacing:
- Cut one 6-inch square for tissue cover top.
- Cut one 23½ x 6¼-inch rectangle for tissue cover sides.

Embroidery

Place 23½ x 6¼-inch side rectangles right side up on flat surface. Measure 6 inches from right short edge and draw a line from the top to the bottom. Measure again 5¾ inches to the left of the first line and draw another vertical line to mark the panel area for embroidery. Embroider 4-inch-high monogram in center of panel using tear-away stabilizer under fabric and rayon machine-embroidery thread.

Assembly

Use ¼-inch-wide seam allowances throughout.

1. Fuse interfacing sides to wrong side of monogrammed fabric sides. With right sides together, sew interfaced sides and lining sides together along upper and side edges. Trim corners and turn right side out.

2. Press edges and fuse lining to interfacing. Butt short edges and whipstitch together using clear monofilament thread. Press corners to form a 5¾ x 5¾-inch box. Glue gimp around lower edge.

3. Fuse top pieces to interfacing top piece. Trace opening template (page 159) onto center of square and cut out through all layers. Glue top to sides, trimming to fit as needed.

4. Glue gimp around opening and top edges of cover.

Jewelry Dish

Cutting

From floral print fabric:

• Cut one 14½ x 2¾-inch rectangle for jewelry dish liner sides.
• Cut one 4¼-inch circle for jewelry dish liner bottom.
• Cut one 15 x ¾-inch strip for jewelry dish lid liner sides.
• Cut one 4½-inch circle for jewelry dish lid liner top.

From coordinating patterned solid fabric:
• Cut one 14½ x 2¾-inch rectangle for jewelry dish sides.
• Cut one 4¼-inch circle for jewelry dish bottom.
• Cut one 15 x ¾-inch strip for jewelry dish lid sides.
• Cut one 6-inch square for jewelry dish lid top.
Note: *Depending on the size of hoop, embroidery for dish lid top may need to be done before cutting.*

From interfacing:
• Cut one 14½ x 2¾-inch rectangle for jewelry dish sides.
• Cut one 4¼-inch circle for jewelry dish bottom.
• Cut one 15 x ¾-inch strip for jewelry dish lid sides.
• Cut one 4½-inch circle for jewelry dish lid top.

Embroidery

Embroider a 2-inch-high monogram in the center of the 6-inch square using tear-away stabilizer under fabric and rayon machinery-embroidery thread. When complete, cut top into a 4½-inch circle with monogram centered.

Assembly

1. Fuse interfacing sides to wrong side of fabric sides. With right sides together, sew liner sides to fused sides along both short and one long edge. Trim corners; turn right side out.

2. Press, fusing lining fabric to interfacing. Overlap short edges to make a 4-inch-diameter circle. Glue overlap in place.

3. Fuse wrong sides of bottom and liner bottom to interfacing. Glue to bottom of sides. Glue gimp over bottom edge.

4. Fuse wrong sides of lid top and lid liner top to interfacing.

5. Assemble lid sides in same manner as bottom sides (steps 1 and 2), making sure lid sides fit over bottom sides before gluing in place.

6. Glue lid top to lid sides. Glue gimp over top edge of lid. Glue tassel trim around lid sides.

Coaster

Cutting
From floral print fabric:
• Cut one 4½-inch square.

From coordinating patterned solid fabric:
• Cut one 4½-inch square.

From interfacing:
• Cut one 4½-inch square.

Assembly

1. Fuse wrong sides of 4½-inch squares of fabric for coasters to interfacing square. Trim corners to round slightly.

2. Glue gimp over edge. ○

Sources: *Fabrics from Waverly Fabrics; stiff double-sided interfacing from Fast2Fuse; gimp and tassel trim from Expo International.*

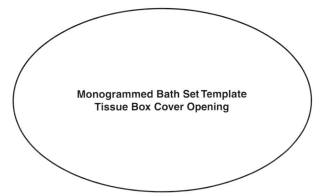

Monogrammed Bath Set Template
Tissue Box Cover Opening

Sew Simple Curtain

Design by Phyllis Dobbs

Keep out the winter chill with a quick-to-sew window panel made with insulated fireproof batting. Designed to hang on a curtain rod, you can cut, sew and install this window treatment in a weekend for an updated look.

Estimated Time
3 hours

Curtain

Finished size
28 x 45¾ inches, including tabs

Materials
- 1 yard 44/45-inch-wide large-print stripe fabric for center panel
- ⅓ yard 44/45-inch-wide contrasting print fabric for inner borders
- ½ yard 44/45-inch-wide coordinating print for outer borders and triangle points
- ¼ yard 44/45-inch-wide coordinating small print fabric for tabs
- 1 yard 44/45-inch-wide contrasting small print fabric for backing
- 1 yard flame-retardant batting
- Basic sewing supplies and equipment

Cutting
From large-print stripe fabric for center panel:
- Cut one 18½ x 29-inch rectangle.

From contrasting print fabric for inner borders:
- Cut two 2½ x 29-inch strips for sides.
- Cut two 2½ x 22½-inch strips for top and bottom.

From coordinating print fabric for outer borders and triangle points:
- Cut two 3½ x 33-inch strips for sides.
- Cut one 3½ x 28½-inch strip for top.
- Using template provided on page 163, cut eight triangle points.

From coordinating small print fabric for tabs:
- Cut six 4½ x 6½-inch pieces.

Assembly
Use ¼-inch-wide seam allowances throughout. Sew right sides together.

Note: *Refer to Assembly Diagram on page 162 throughout.*

1. Sew side inner borders to center panel; sew top and bottom inner borders to center panel unit.

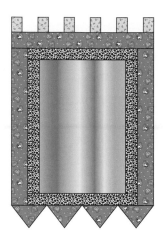

Sew Simple Curtain
Assembly Diagram

2. Repeat step 1 with sides and top border to complete curtain front.

3. Sew triangle points together in pairs, leaving top edge open. Trim seams at tips. Turn right side out and press. Set aside.

4. Fold tabs in half lengthwise and sew side edges together. Turn right side out and press with seam centered in the middle of tab.

5. Cut backing and batting to fit curtain front. Place backing right side up. Fold tabs in half with seam inside the fold; beginning ¼ inch from one

edge, position tabs evenly spaced along top edge of backing with raw edges even.

6. Pin triangle points along bottom edge of backing with raw edges even. Position curtain with right sides together. Place batting on wrong side of curtain front. Pin all layers together.

7. Position curtain layers with batting on top for sewing. Sew layers together, leaving a 6-inch opening on one side. Turn right side out and press, pulling tabs and points out. Whipstitch opening closed. ⏱

Sources: *Sweetheart Ballerinas fabric designed by Phyllis Dobbs, available from Quilting Treasures; Warm & Safe flame-retardant batting from The Warm Company; Coats Dual Duty XP all-purpose thread from Coats & Clark.*

Quick Tip

To adapt this pattern for a matching valance, determine the height of the valance including the tabs and subtract that measurement from center panel and side borders when cutting.

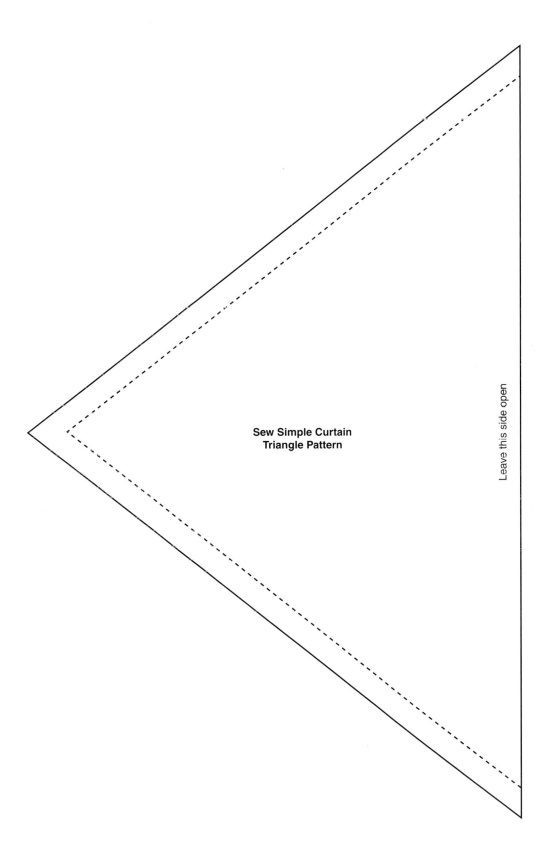

**Sew Simple Curtain
Triangle Pattern**

Leave this side open

Simple-to-Quilt Chair Cover

Design by Phyllis Dobbs

When investing in new chairs is out of the question, try these simple-to-quilt covers to dress up everyday chairs. These are "sew" simple to quilt you'll want to make a set for every holiday.

Estimated Time
2 hours

Chair Cover

Finished size
12½ x 17½ inches (folded)

Materials
- 44/45-inch-wide cotton fabric:
    - ¼ yard pink floral
    - ⅓ yard pink stripe
    - 1¼ yards dark pink tonal
- Lightweight cotton batting
- Basic sewing supplies and equipment

Cutting
From pink floral fabric:
- Use template on page 167 to cut four B triangles.

From pink stripe fabric:
- Use template to cut four A triangles.
- Cut four 1½ x 13-inch strips.

From dark pink tonal fabric:
- Cut four 2½ x 11-inch strips.
- Cut four 3 x 13-inch strips.
- Cut four 2 x 19-inch strips.

Assembly

Use ¼-inch-wide seam allowances throughout. Sew right sides together. Press seams as you sew, pressing toward darker fabric.

Note: *Refer to Assembly Diagram throughout.*

Simple-to-Quilt Chair Cover
Assembly Diagram

1. Sew an A triangle to a B triangle, joining on diagonal edges. Repeat to join remaining A and B triangles. Join A/B units in pairs to make two center squares.

2. Sew 2½ x 11-inch dark pink tonal strips on each side of center squares. Sew a 1½ x 13-inch stripe strip across top and bottom edges.

3. Sew 3 x 13-inch dark pink tonal strips across top and bottom edges of units. Sew the two pieced units together to complete the pieced top.

4. For tie, fold a 2 x 19-inch dark pink tonal strip in half with right sides together. Sew long edges together, leaving one end open. Repeat with remaining three 2 x 19-inch strips. Turn right side out and press.

5. Place the pieced top on dark pink tonal fabric, right sides together. Place these layers on top of batting and pin together. Cut dark pink tonal fabric and batting to match top unit.

6. Insert open end of tie between the two layers of fabric at each bottom side corner, aligning end of tie with side edge of fabric. Pin edges.

7. Sew front and back pieces together, leaving a 5-inch opening on one edge. Trim corners; turn right side out. Sew opening closed.

8. Baste layers together and quilt ⅛ inch from seam lines of all pieces. ⏱

Sources: *Warm & Natural cotton batting from The Warm Company; Coats Dual Duty XP all-purpose thread from Coats & Clark.*

Quick Tip

To adjust the pattern for a wider chair back, divide the additional width by 2 and add to each of the side borders. Lengthen the crosswise strips by this amount also.

To lengthen the chair back cover, determine the additional amount needed and divide by 4. Add this amount to the top and bottom dark pink borders.

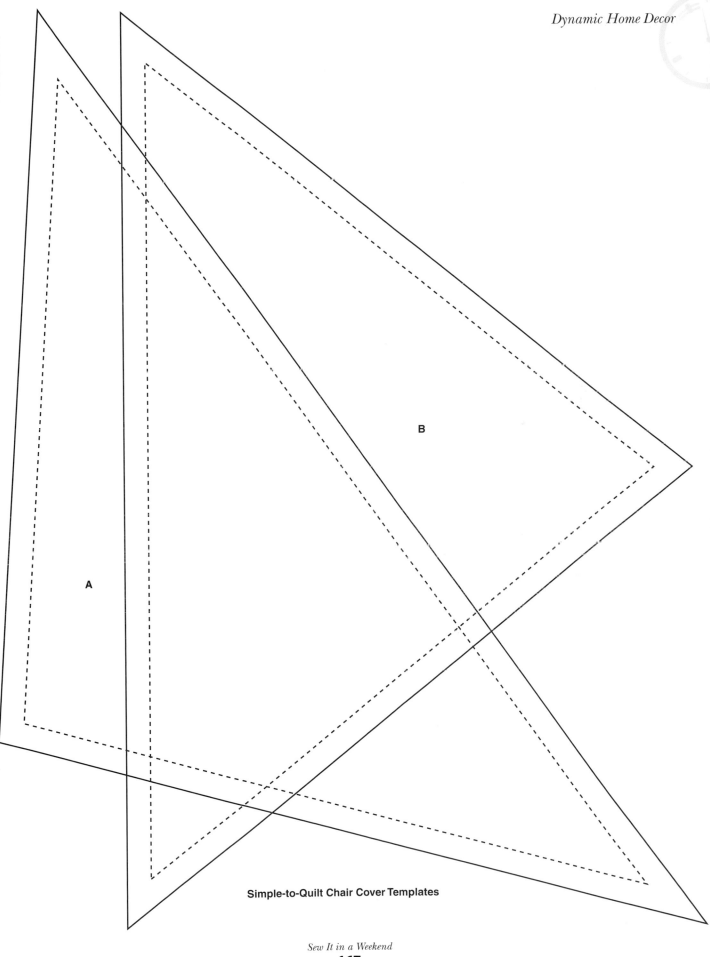

A

B

Simple-to-Quilt Chair Cover Templates

Sleepy-Time Yo-Yo Bedding

Design by Patsy Moreland

Bedtime is a time of relaxation, and what better way to relax than in these pretty yo-yo-embellished sheets. Yo-yos are a great way to use up scrap fabric to enhance wearables and home decor. Be careful; once you start, you'll never want to stop!

Estimated Time
6 hours

Bedding

Finished size
Yo-yos fit 2 pillowcases and 1 flat sheet

Materials
- ¼ yard each variety of printed cotton/cotton blend fabrics
- 2 pillowcases
- 1 flat bed sheet
- Quilting thread
- 8½ x 11-inch template plastic or freezer paper
- Basic sewing supplies and equipment

Preparation
1. Wash, dry and steam-press fabrics, sheet and pillowcases.

2. Cut a 3¼- and 2½-inch circle from template plastic or freezer paper.

Yo-Yos
1. Cutting through three layers of fabric at a time, cut a total of 18 (3¼-inch) A circles and 41 (2½-inch) B circles from printed cotton fabrics.

2. For each yo-yo, fold edge of circle under ¼ inch. Using a single strand of quilting thread, hand-stitch around folded edge (Figure 1).

Figure 1

3. Pull thread ends to gather yo-yo into a bundle and tie ends together. Cut thread ends 1 inch above knot. Stuff thread ends through gathered hole opening.

4. Steam-press yo-yo so hole is centered on one side.

Assembly

1. Using an air-soluble marker or basting stitches, mark the center length and width of borders on pillowcases and sheet (Figure 2).

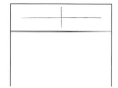

Figure 2

2. Pin one large (A) yo-yo in center of border. Referring to Figure 3, add additional yo-yos. Continue in this pattern to pin yo-yos across borders of pillowcases and sheet.

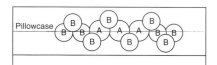

Figure 3

3. Hand-stitch yo-yos in place using all-purpose thread and small stitches. ⏱

Quick Tip

For added embellishment, embroider lazy-daisy flowers with French-knot accents between yo-yos, and sew decorative buttons as centers over some of the yo-yos.

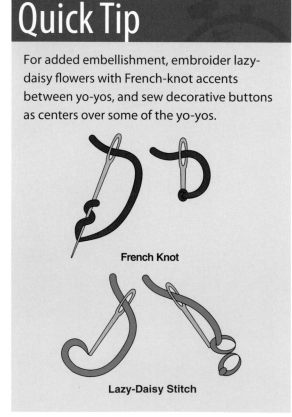

French Knot

Lazy-Daisy Stitch

Quick Tip

Place a piece of ¼-inch-wide masking tape in the center of your thumbnail of your non-sewing hand. It makes a great guide when turning under yo-yo seam allowances.

Romantic Canopy Cover

Design by Pamela Hastings

Your bedroom is your refuge, and a bed canopy can add just the right amount of cozy glamour to your room. In a child's room, this canopy can make any little girl feel like a princess. Basic curtain rods and coordinating fabrics in colors you love are all you need to turn your bed into a glamorous retreat.

Estimated Time
5 hours

Canopy

Finished sizes
Valance: 104 x 17½ inches*
Side Panel: 40½ x 86 inches*
Back Panel: 90 x 86 inches*
Before gathering

Materials
- 54-inch-wide decorator fabric:
    - 6½ yards floral for valance and side panels
    - 11½ yards coordinating floral for back panel and side panel lining
    - 2 yards stripe for valance lining and trim
- 1 (2-inch-wide) valance rod with 6–7-inch clearance
- 1 (¾-inch-wide) sash rod
- 4½ yards shirring tape
- Self-adhesive hook-and-loop tape
- Basic sewing supplies and equipment

Project note: *Canopy will fit a 36-inch-wide twin-size bed.*

Cutting

From floral fabric for valance and side panels:
• Cut to make a 108 x 17-inch strip for valance, piecing as needed.
• Cut two 40 x 87-inch pieces for side panels.

From coordinating floral fabric for back panel and side panel lining:
• Cut to make a 94 x 91-inch rectangle for back panel, piecing as needed.
• Cut two 40 x 87-inch rectangles for side panel lining.

From striped fabric for valance lining and trim:
• Cut to make a 108 x 21-inch strip for valance lining, piecing as needed.
• Cut two 4 x 87-inch strips for side panel trim, piecing as needed.

Valance Assembly

Use ½-inch seam allowances unless otherwise noted. Sew with right sides together.

1. With raw edges even, sew valance and valance lining pieces together along both long edges. Press seams open. Turn right side out.

2. Press valance so that top edge of lining and valance are even and lining forms a 1½-inch band along the bottom edge (Figure 1).

Figure 1

3. On side seams on valance, turn under a 1-inch fold and press. Top stitch into place.

4. Cut a length of shirring tape 1 inch longer than the width of the valance. Pin the tape in place along the top edge on the lining side of the valance ½ inch from the top. Turn under the cut edges of the tape and stitch tape in place close to the top and bottom edges (Figure 2).

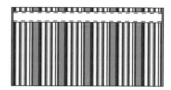

Figure 2

5. Tie the strings together at one end of the valance, and pull the remaining string ends to shirr the valance.

Side Panel Assembly

Use ½-inch seam allowances unless otherwise noted. Sew with right sides together.

1. With raw edges even, sew one side-panel-trim strip to the right-hand edge of one side panel. Pin remaining edge of the trim strip to the left-hand edge of the side-panel lining (Figure 3). Stitch in place and press seam allowances toward trim.

Figure 3

2. Repeat with second side panel, attaching trim to the left-hand side of the panel and the right-hand side of the panel lining.

3. Pin each panel/panel lining unit with right sides together and raw edges even along the top, bottom and side edges. Stitch, leaving an opening in the top edge for turning.

4. Trim corners diagonally and turn panel right side out. Press. Slipstitch opening closed.

5. Cut a length of shirring tape 1 inch longer than the width of the completed side panel. Refer to steps 4 and 5 of Valance Assembly to sew tape in place and shirr panels.

Back Panel Assembly

Use ½-inch seam allowances unless otherwise noted. Sew with right sides together.

1. Turn under and press a 1½-inch double hem at bottom of back panel. Stitch in place.

2. Turn under and press a 1-inch double hem along each side. Stitch in place.

3. Edge finish remaining raw edge. Turn top edge under 2 inches and press. Stitch 1½ inches from folded edge to form casing.

Hanging Instructions

1. Hang valance rod brackets so the bottom edge of the bracket is 86 inches above the floor and 2 inches outside the sides of the bed (Figure 4).

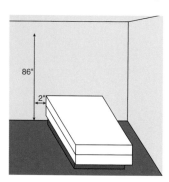

Figure 4

2. Hang the sash rod brackets between the valance rod brackets. Insert sash rod into the casing of the back panel and hang back panel.

3. Attach valance rod to the brackets. Cut two strips of hook-and-loop tape the measurement of the valance rod clearance. Remove backing and attach to the *inside* of the rod along the bracket, ½ inch from the top. Adjust gathers on side panels and attach the loop side of the tape over the shirring tape on the side panels.

4. Cut a strip of hook-and-loop tape equal to the outside of the valance rod and the outside edge of the valance clearance. Remove backing from hook side of tape and attach to the *outside* of the rod ½ inch below the top. Adjust gathers on valance and attach the loop side of the tape over the shirring tape on the valance.

5. Attach the side panels to the inside of the valance rod on the hook tape. Attach valance to the outside of the rod. ⏱

Special Thanks

Please join us in thanking the talented designers listed below for creating these fabulous, fun to sew projects created in six hours or less.

Susan Breier
Glowing Sweatshirt Redo, 50

Janis Bullis
On the Go Laptop Cover, 60
Wine Caddy, 98

Denise Clason
A Snowy Welcome, 68

Holly Daniels
Cherish the Moment Journal, 110

Phyllis Dobbs
Sew Simple Curtain, 160
Simple-to-Quilt Chair Cover, 164

Zoe Graul
Be Cozy Felted Tea Cozy, 100
Over-the-Top Denim, 26

Linda Turner Griepentrog
Celebrate Denim Jacket, 22
It's All Black & White, 57
Sophisticated Soap, 104

Leslie Hartsock
Tumbling Blocks Blanket, 73

Pamela Hastings
Hideaway Shelving Unit, 149
Romantic Canopy Cover, 171

June McCrary Jacobs
On the Roll Checkers Game, 80

Pam Lindquist for Coats & Clark
Leaf Peeper's Tote, 84

Chris Malone
Porcelain Pincushion, 124
Sew Fun Sewing Basket, 119
Update Your Denim Skirt, 30

Dorothy Martin
Stole the Show Shawl, 18

Lorine Mason
Apron Duo, 7
Reading Wrap, 11

Agnes Mercik
Luxury Bath Ensemble, 152

Patsy Moreland
Sleepy-Time Yo-Yo Bedding, 168

Karen Neary
Pearl Needlework Set, 114

Bev Shenefield
Standing Room Only Stadium Jacket, 47

Missy Shepler
Autumn Print T-Shirt, 34
Express Yourself, 64

Paula Smith-Danell
Pop Art Handkerchief Top, 14

Cheryl Stranges
No-Sweat Work-Out Mat, 76

Lynn Weglarz
Fuzzy Fleecy Fun Neckwear, 44
Top Off Your T-Shirt, 41

Angie Wilhite
Calm Cat Neck Wrap, 89
I Love Golf & Bowling, 92
Sachet Heart Appliqué Bags, 107

Shelia Zent
At-the-Knee Jeans, 38

Carol Zentgraf
Fat-Quarter Duvet Cover, 146
Flowers & Stripes Tablecloth, 139
Just-Like-New Seat Cushions, 144
Kit & Caboodle Kitchen Towels, 95
Monogrammed Bath Set, 156
One-Step-Up Footstool, 129
Simply Striped Pillow Trio, 132
Trapunto Table Topper, 143
"What in the World"
   Table-Panel Shower Curtain, 136

Sewing Basket

Basic Sewing Tools & Equipment

- Sewing machine and matching thread
- Serger, if desired
- Scissors of various sizes, including pinking shears
- Rotary cutter(s), mats and straightedges
- Pattern tracing paper or cloth
- Pressing tools such as sleeve rolls and June Tailor boards
- Pressing equipment, including ironing board and iron; press cloths

- Straight pins and pin cushion
- Measuring tools
- Marking pens (either air- or water-soluble) or tailor's chalk
- Spray adhesive (temporary)
- Hand-sewing needles and thimble
- Point turners

Sewing Sources

The following companies provided fabric and/or supplies for projects in this book. If you are unable to locate a product locally, contact the manufacturers listed below for the closest retail or mail-order source.

Beacon Adhesives Inc.
(914) 699-3405
www.beaconcreates.com

Blick Art Supplies
(800) 828-4548
www.dickblick.com

Blue Moon Beads
(800) 377-6715
www.bluemoonbeads.com

Clover Needlecraft Inc.
(800) 233-1703
www.clover-usa.com

Coats & Clark
(800) 648-1479
www.coatsandclark.com

Darice
(866) 432-7423
www.darice.com

Dharma Trading Co.
(800) 542-5227
www.dharmatrading.com

Dill Buttons of America Inc.
(888) 462-8555
www.dill-buttons.com.

DMC
(973) 589-0606
www.dmc-usa.com

Drapery Sewing Supplies
(800) 314-6270
www.draperysewing
supplies.com

Expo International
(800) 542-4367
www.expointl.com

Fairfield Processing
(800) 980-8000
www.poly-fil.com

Fast 2 Fuse
(800) 284-1114
www.fast2fuse.com

French Connections
(919) 545-9296
www.French-nc.com

Husqvarna Viking
www.husqvarnaviking.com

Jacquard Products: Rupert, Gibbon & Spider Inc.
(800) 442-0455
www.jacquardproducts.com

Kandi Corp.
(800) 985-2634
www.kandicorp.com

Michael Miller Fabrics
(212) 704-0774
www.michaelmiller
fabrics.com

Perfect Little Stitches
www.perfectlittle
stitches.com

Pellon Consumer Products
(800) 223-5275
www.pellonideas.com

Prym Consumer USA Inc.
www.prymdritz.com

Quilting Treasures
(800) 876-2756
www.quiltingtreasures.com

Smart Needle
(248) 807-8726
www.smartneedle.com

Sulky of America
(800) 874-4115
www.sulky.com

Therm O Web
(847) 520-5200
www.thermoweb.com

Thibaut Fabrics
(800) 223-0704
www.thibautdesign.com

Warm Company (The)
(425) 248-2424
www.warmcompany.com

Waverly Fabrics
www.waverly.com

Windham Fabrics
(866) 842-7631
www.windhamfabrics.com

This book is enhanced by the product support of tools and supplies, provided to our designers by the vendors listed on this page.